AMERICAN POETS PROJECT

AMERICAN POETS PROJECT

IS PUBLISHED WITH A GIFT IN MEMORY OF

James Merrill

AND SUPPORT FROM ITS FOUNDING PATRONS

Sidney J. Weinberg, Jr. Foundation

The Berkley Foundation

Richard B. Fisher and Jeanne Donovan Fisher

Muriel Rukeyser

selected poems

adrienne rich editor

AMERICAN POETS PROJECT

THE LIBRARY OF AMERICA

Introduction, volume compilation, and notes copyright © 2004 by Literary Classics of the United States, Inc. All rights reserved. Printed in the United States of America. No part of this book may be reproduced in any manner whatsoever without permission.

Copyright © 1935, 1938, 1939, 1944, 1948, 1958, 1962, 1968, 1973, 1976, 1978 by Muriel Rukeyser. Reprinted by permission of William Rukeyser. Quotations from *The Life of Poetry* in the Introduction reprinted with permission of Paris Press (Ashfield, MA), copyright © William Rukeyser.

The paper used in this publication meets the minimum requirements of the American National Standard for Information Sciences—Permanence of Paper for Printed Library Materials, ANSI Z39.48—1984.

Design by Chip Kidd and Mark Melnick.
Frontispiece courtesy Library of Congress.

Library of Congress Cataloging-in-Publication Data:
Rukeyser, Muriel, 1913–1980
[Poems. Selections]
Selected poems / Muriel Rukeyser ; Adrienne Rich, editor.
     p. cm. — (American poets project ; 9)
Includes index.
Contents: From Theory of flight (1935) — From U.S. 1 (1938) — From A turning wind (1939) — From Beast in view (1944) — From The green wave (1948) — From Body of waking (1958) — From Waterlily fire (1962) — From The speed of darkness (1968) — From Breaking open (1973) — From The gates (1976).
ISBN 1–931082–58–8 (alk. paper)
   I. Rich, Adrienne Cecile. II. Title. III. Series.
PS3535.U4A6 2004
811'.52 — dc22
2003060484

10 9 8 7 6 5 4 3 2 1

Muriel
Rukeyser

CONTENTS

INTRODUCTION

Muriel Rukeyser was a major and prolific American poet and writer, and through most of her life a political and cultural activist. Besides her 573-page *Collected Poems*, she left behind three biographies; a musical play, *Houdini*; a quite unclassifiable, mesmerizing narrative called *The Orgy*; translations from the Mexican poet Octavio Paz and the Swedish poet Gunnar Ekelöf; *The Life of Poetry*, a study of poetics and social crisis; and still uncollected essays, journalism, letters, film-scripts, and plays. Her reputation has endured many pendulum swings in her lifetime and beyond; she has not been easy to assess or appropriate in the ways that many poets are packaged for consumption. Her breadth of concern with the world was large, her issues and literary techniques many, and she refused to compartmentalize herself or her work, claiming her right to intellect and sexuality, poetry and science, Marxism and myth, activism and motherhood, theory and vision. None of these were scattershot "phases," for she was one of the great integrators, seeing the fragmentary world of modernity not as irretrievably broken, but in need of societal and emotional repair.

Born in 1913 "in the first century of world wars," Rukeyser grew up in New York City as the elder daughter of secular Jewish parents from Yonkers and Milwaukee, on the cusp of prosperity: her mother a onetime bookkeeper and her father a concrete salesman who became a partner in a sand and gravel company. The city itself was growing around her by means of hand-thrown fiery rivets, poured cement, huge machines, intensive development. "Each of these apartment houses, standing like dead trunks along the avenue, has its army of children." Around them, "The city rises in its light. Skeletons of buildings; the orange-peel cranes; highways put through; the race of skyscrapers. And you are a part of this."

There were nannies, a chauffeur-driven car, upwardly mobile aspirations. "I was expected to grow up and become a golfer"—a suburban professional's wife. Books and the arts were regarded as decoration, but good education provided: private schooling, Vassar College for two years. A downturn in the family fortunes after the economic crash of 1929 caused her to leave Vassar and conventional formal education. The girl being readied for successful matronhood was from a young age a reader, an explorer of the city with the children's gangs in her neighborhood, and a secret writer of poems before she knew there were living poets. ("All are dead; the musicians, the poets, the sculptors. This is a world of business. Real men go to the office.") And "it was clear to a growing child that the terrible, murderous differences between the ways people lived were being upheld all over the city . . ."

Muriel Rukeyser was a new kind of American, intensely and for her entire life identified with one city, yet internationalist in her spirit and actions; journeying world-wide yet rooted. Her poetry embraces both New York, which in some poems becomes virtually part of her body, and places whose conflicts and configurations entered her psyche: Gauley Bridge, West Virginia; Catalonia during the Spanish Civil War; the Outer Banks; the Ajanta Caves in India; Ireland; Vietnam; South Korea.

Few American poets have understood as Rukeyser did how the individual life, even if unconscious or apathetic to the fact, is shaped in history and in collectivity. She created a poetics of historical sensibility—not as nostalgia but as resource to express and interpret contemporary experience and imagine a different future.

> Organize the full results of that rich past
> open the windows : potent catalyst

she wrote at twenty in "Poem Out of Childhood." Here, as throughout her work, the poet's personal memories are knitted together with politics. The word "organize" is significant here, in its activist connotation but even more in its sense of dynamic relational system, a concept that would become crucial to her art and thought.

Her first published poems, in a Vassar undergraduate magazine, invoke New York City scenes and conversations:

"Look," the city child said, "they have built over the river.
It is a lovely curve. But think what that might be:
A circle on that arch would be really something to see!—"

The toll-taker heard, and grinned, and spat. "Lord, what
       a kid!"
Like them all,—wants a good thing to go on and on
       forever.
Tell him he ought to be glad they made what they did."

Made what they did! . . . I saw the bridge built. One
    spring
A riveter stood high on the iron skeleton
And the flakes of white fire fell and his hard face shone.

Men strung out cables. They were beautiful,
Cables and men, hard, polished, gleaming,—
The pride that the man-work should now prove fruitful!

The states send automobiles over the Hudson River.
A man stands on the abyss, dropping a penny down,
Breathlessly watching the rush. Stand. The lights of the
    town

Shine down the Drive, and the grim towers of empire
Are bright, burst, to kindle the evening; the torches shiver,
Flaming high, whirling the city into one strong wind of fire.

Already, despite awkward phrasings, salient qualities of her
work are present: the sense of the great made structures
of modernity, creations both of technology and of human
manual labor; of the makers themselves, and also the mi-
nute individual figure against the finished structure. And
the child's imagination wanting more. Rukeyser had
watched the building of the George Washington Bridge as
she was driven back and forth to school along Riverside
Drive. She saw it as the consummation of a process, but
also as itself altering both the city and the lives of people, of
the states beyond the city. She was soon to travel into those
states, and further.

A brief account of the events of her life can only sug-
gest the range and depths they took her to. Both before
and after leaving Vassar she took summer courses at Co-
lumbia in psychology and anthropology; she was already

involved in the vibrant though far from unanimous circles of the Left in New York, "at the center of a decade," Suzanne Gardinier observes, "whose integration of matters literary and political many of us now can scarcely imagine." She was writing for various periodicals including *The Daily Worker*, *The New Republic*, *New Masses*, taking part in the debates of the Left, communist and socialist, Stalinist and Leninist and Trotskyist—and artistic. "Three Sides of a Coin" in her first book evokes—and interrogates—the mixture of sensual, emotional, and intellectual life in this period.

In 1933 she received ground flight training at an aviation school (a minor, she needed parental permission to train as a pilot, which was denied). In the same year she traveled to Scottsboro, Alabama, to report on a historic case in which nine African-American youths were convicted of raping two white women (a conviction later overturned by the Supreme Court and a landmark issue for the Left). There she was jailed for fraternizing with other journalists across racial lines, and contracted typhoid fever. At the age of 21 she received the Yale Series of Younger Poets Award for her first book, *Theory of Flight*.

The assurance of voice and materials in this book, its ambition and scope, ran formidably counter to existing traditions of feminine lyricism as represented by Edna St. Vincent Millay, Elinor Wylie, Louise Bogan, or even Lola Ridge and Marya Zaturenska, women poets born in the nineteenth century and writing into the twentieth. In the words of Louise Kertesz, her first critic-in-depth: "No woman poet made the successful fusion of personal and social themes in a modern prosody before Rukeyser." She was also a breakaway from the irony and fatalism of such modernists as Eliot and Auden. The young Rukeyser entered, rather, into the company of Whitman, Crane, and, as Reginald Gibbons has noted, Thomas McGrath. She also knew her Bible and Shakespeare, and other English poets of the past: "*Think:* poems fixed this landscape: Blake, Donne, Keats." In *Theory of Flight*, and in the book that followed three years later, *U.S. 1*, she was already in full possession of her poetic powers and her cohering, though variously embodied, world-view. And already, though by nature she rejected the feminine tradition, she was writing as a woman, a fully sexual human being.

In an essay written in 1944 for the *Contemporary Jewish Record* she asserts:

> To live as poet, woman, American, and Jew—this chalks in my position. If the four come together in one person, each strengthens the other . . .

but she also delineates her conflict with the social and political timidity of the Jewish world in which she grew up, and her choice of the Jewish ethic she voices in part VII of "Letter to the Front":

> To be a Jew in the twentieth century
> Is to be offered a gift. If you refuse,
> Wishing to be invisible, you choose
> Death of the spirit, the stone insanity.
> Accepting, take full life. Full agonies:
> Your evening deep in labyrinthine blood
> Of those who resist, fail, and resist: and God
> Reduced to a hostage among hostages.
>
> The gift is torment. Not alone the still
> Torture, isolation; or torture of the flesh.
> That may come also. But the accepting wish,
> The whole and fertile spirit as guarantee
> For every human freedom, suffering to be free,
> Daring to live for the impossible.

Published in 1944, the poem reflects on the temptation "to be invisible" offered American Jews even as, in the Warsaw Ghetto, other Jews were resisting, failing, "suffering to be free."

From the first, she was also intensely committed to poetic craft, refusing to allow political awareness to shoulder it out. Tim Dayton, in his study of "The Book of the Dead," notes, "This concern about developing a command of poetic technique, and that political concerns and consciousness not become a substitute for it, runs through Rukeyser's correspondence of the 1930s and 1940s."

In 1936 she made two very different though interrelated journeys—to Gauley Bridge in West Virginia, site of the (then) worst industrial disaster in American history, and to Barcelona to cover the anti-Fascist "People's Olympics." Turned away from Spain as the Fascists were prevailing, she experienced enough there—including love for an anti-Fascist German athlete who remained to fight and die in Spain—to crystallize her political vision. As she described it years later:

> I wanted very much for the Communist Party, as I invented it, as I thought of it, to be something that I could be close to, but I was unable to do that . . . the thing that I wanted most, was the United Front, and I saw that in the first days of the Spanish Civil War, not in Spain proper, but in Catalonia, where socialists, anarchists, Communists, trade unions and gypsies were together in a United Front.

If the Communist Party U.S.A. was too narrow, too doctrinaire for her, the greater vistas of a humanist Marxism were not, and as Dayton has shown in a close and critical reading, they deeply inform the central poem of *U.S. 1*, "The Book of the Dead." I would add that they continued to inform her work throughout her life, expressed in her own language.

The next few years found her in San Francisco for the opening of the Golden Gate Bridge, teaching at the California Labor School, writing articles and poetry reviews, working on a biography of the first American physicist, Willard Gibbs, giving at Vassar and elsewhere the lectures that were to become *The Life of Poetry*. Disinherited by her family, she had a two-month, annulled marriage, bore a son by a different man, and raised him as a single mother. She edited a brief-lived "review of Free Culture" called *Decision*, was witch-hunted as a Communist, was attacked and caricatured by both conservative and "proletarian" literary critics (and praised by poets as unlike as Kenneth Rexroth and May Swenson), and went into psychoanalysis with the Jungian analyst Frances Wickes. She wrote a biography of the defeated Republican candidate for President, Wendell Willkie, and of the English Renaissance scientist Thomas Hariot. She started teaching regularly in 1954 at Sarah Lawrence College, suffered several strokes (see "The Resurrection of the Right Side" and "The Wards"), participated in the anti-war actions of the Vietnam era, traveled to Vietnam during the bombing of Hanoi with the poet Denise Levertov, and, as president of the American P.E.N. International Center, to South Korea, where she stood vigil before the prison of a communist poet incarcerated for his writings. She lived to see her poetry rediscovered by a younger generation of politicized women poets and readers, and her *Collected Poems* in print. Because she had always pursued a complex and open political vision, she never joined the ranks of disillusioned or right-veering Left intellectuals and artists, even in periods when (as in the late 1940s and 50s) there was little public resonance for her sense of "the truths of outrage and the truths of possibility."

Rukeyser's *The Life of Poetry* (1949; reprinted by Paris Press in 1996) is a study of the function of poetry in a time of crisis, an examination of "the outcast art" as a wasted elemental resource in American life. "American poetry," she says, "has been part of a culture in conflict."

> . . . We are a people tending toward democracy at the level of hope; on another level, the economy of the nation, the empire of business within the republic, both include in their basic premise the concept of perpetual warfare. It is the history of the idea of war that is beneath our other histories. . . . But around and under and above it is another reality . . . This history is the history of possibility.

Unlike certain essays by poets deploring the marginality of poetry, this is not the complaint of a dissatisfied ego, nor is it the defense of an elite art against the threat of burial by mass or popular culture. It is, rather, a reflection on our social history and literature in terms of "the buried, the lost and the wasted" and the denial of vital relationships in defining who we are as a people. It's an argument against the reification of poetry, whether as iconic or irrelevant; she takes poetry out from the static into the dynamic:

> . . . [A] poem is not its words or its images, any more than a symphony is its notes or a river its drops of water. Poetry depends on the moving relations within itself. It is an art that lives in time, expressing and evoking the moving relation between the individual consciousness and the world. The work that a

poem does is transfer of human energy, and I think
human energy may be defined as consciousness, the
capacity to make change in existing conditions.

She identifies "the fear of poetry" as resistance to such ex-
changes of energy, such potential—a resistance she traces
in American history, in the early colonists' fear of ques-
tioning beliefs and divisions brought from the old world,
the fear of "foreignness" and strangeness among offspring
of post-immigrant generations, and in "the use of the dis-
coveries of science rather than the methods of science."
Science in its methods pursues relationships and flows of
energy, though its products, technology, have been wor-
shipped (and commoditized) without understanding of
those methods. For Rukeyser a poem is a system of
"moving relations" among words, images, sounds: "a web
of movement," not of "static mechanics" as she describes
the analytic method of the New Critics:

> The use of language involves symbols so general, so
> dense emotionally, that the life of the symbols them-
> selves must continually be taken into consideration.
> In poetry, the relations are not formed like crystals
> on a lattice of words . . . Poetry is to be regarded ac-
> cording to a very different set of laws . . .

In considering poetic thinking, like scientific method, as
one of the essential elements of human power, insepara-
ble from the re-making of society, she goes far beyond
any narrow argumentation for or against "political poetry."
She does not need to say, nor does she, "all poetry is
political."

If Rukeyser had left us only "The Book of the Dead"
and *The Life of Poetry*, she would have made a remarkable

contribution to American literature. But the range and daring of her work, its generosity of vision, its formal innovations, and its level of energy are unequalled among twentieth-century American poets. Her poems can be panoramic (yet vividly concrete), intimate, epigrammatic, meditative, sensual, mordantly witty, visionary; never are they quiescent or disenchanted. She wrote of sexuality before feminism and gay liberation cleared the space for new sexual honesties, as in poems such as her 1938 "Girl at the Play":

Long after you beat back the powerful hand
and leave the scene, prison's still there to break.
Brutalized by escape, you travel out to sit
in empty theatres, your stunned breast, hardened neck
    waiting for warmth to venture back.

Gilded above the stage, staring archaic shapes
hang, like those men you learn submission from
whose majesty sits yellow on the night,
young, indolent girls, long-handed, one's vague mouth
    and cruel nose and jaw and throat.

Waiting's paralysis strikes, king-cobra hooded head's
infected fangs petrify body and face.
emblems fade everyway, dissolving even
the bitter infantile boys who call for sleep's
    winy breasts whose nipples are long grapes.

Seats fill. The curtain's up where strong lights act,
cut theatre to its theme, the quick fit's past.
Here's answer in masses moving, by light elect,
they turn the stage before into the street behind,
    and nothing's so forgotten as your blind
    female paralysis that takes the mind,

>and nothing's so forgotten as your dead
>fever, now that it's past and the swift play's ahead.

Thousands of poems by women, worldwide, have ended in passive posture, in "waiting's paralysis"; this girl escapes submission into the quickened life of art, of a theater moreover where "they turn the stage before into the street behind." And I would add that this is not only a women's poem; it embodies—through its own language—the power of art to revive spirit, stimulate consciousness, restore a brutalized humanity.

Rukeyser's work, like that of any really far-reaching poet, was uneven; there are, mostly in her later poems, abstract and rhetorical passages, when she seems to run on automatic pilot. Suzanne Gardinier has observed,

>More than most poets in her country, she wrote in dialogue with the history of her time, specifically with the current of hope for change within it; in the poems she wrote . . . [between 1948 and 1968] when her partner's voice became all but inaudible, there is often the rambling hollowness of a conversation of one.

And yet, in that period she was single-handedly raising her son, and writing poems as varied as "Foghorn in Horror" (a shattering depiction of the loss of historical resonance) and "Waterlily Fire":

>Whatever can come to a city can come to this city . . .
>Whatever can happen to a woman can happen to me . . .
>Whatever can happen to anyone can happen to me . . .

—a remarkable intuition for a New Yorker, for a white and middle-class American citizen, in 1958.

■

Reading Muriel Rukeyser, writing about her as I have from time to time, I have come to feel more and more the power of her work and presence in American literature— the many kinds of lives and issues she touched, the silences she broke, the voices she made audible, the landscapes she covered. In our own time of crisis, when the idea of perpetual war has dropped whatever masks it ever wore, when poetry is still feared yet no longer so marginalized, when a late-1920s schoolgirl's perception of the "grim towers of empire" and "the terrible, murderous differences in the way people lived" accord with what more and more people around the world are experiencing and naming, this poet has readers waiting for her who perhaps, holding this book, will be seeing her name for the first time.

Adrienne Rich
August 2003

Note: As I write this, a new and complete collection of Rukeyser's poems is in preparation (edited by Anne Herzog and Janet Kaufman, to be published in the near future by the University of Pittsburgh Press). The first full-length biography is being written by Jan Heller Levi.

Poem Out of Childhood

I

Breathe-in experience, breathe-out poetry   :
Not Angles, angels   :   and the magnificent past
shot deep illuminations into high-school.
I opened the door into the concert-hall
and a rush of triumphant violins answered me
while the syphilitic woman turned her mouldered face
intruding upon Brahms.   Suddenly, in an accident
the girl's brother was killed, but her father had just
        died   :
she stood against the wall, leaning her cheek,
dumbly her arms fell, "What will become of me?" and
I went into the corridor for a drink of water.
These bandages of image wrap my head
when I put my hand up I hardly feel the wounds.
We sat on the steps of the unrented house
raining blood down on Loeb and Leopold,
creating again how they removed his glasses
and philosophically slit his throat.

>   They who manipulated and misused our youth,
>   smearing those centuries upon our hands,

trapping us in a welter of dead names,
snuffing and shaking heads at patent truth. . . .

We were ready to go the long descent with Virgil
the bough's gold shade advancing forever with us,
entering the populated cold of drawing-rooms;
Sappho, with her drowned hair trailing along Greek
     waters,
weed binding it, a fillet of kelp enclosing
the temples' ardent fruit   :

                    Not Sappho, Sacco.
Rebellion pioneered among our lives,
viewing from far-off many-branching deltas,
innumerable seas.

II

In adolescence I knew travellers
speakers digressing from the ink-pocked rooms,
bearing the unequivocal sunny word.

    Prinzip's year bore us   :   see us turning at breast
    quietly while the air throbs over Sarajevo
    after the mechanic laugh of that bullet.
    How could they know what sinister knowledge
        finds
    its way among our brains' wet palpitance,
    what words would nudge and giggle at our spine,
    what murders dance?
    These horrors have approached the growing child;
    now that the factory is sealed-up brick

the kids throw stones, smashing the windows,
membranes of uselessness in desolation.

We grew older quickly, watching the father shave
and the splatter of lather hardening on the glass,
playing in sandboxes to escape paralysis,
being victimized by fataller sly things.
"Oh, and you," he said, scraping his jaw, "what will
    you be?"
"Maybe : something : like : Joan : of
    : Arc. . . ."
Allies Advance, we see,
Six Miles South to Soissons.   And we beat the
    drums.
Watchsprings snap in the mind, uncoil, relax,
the leafy years all somber with foreign war.
How could we know what exposed guts resembled?

A wave, shocked to motion, babbles margins
from Asia to Far Rockaway spiralling
among clocks in its four-dimensional circles.
Disturbed by war we pedalled bicycles
breakneck down the decline, until the treads
conquered our speed and pulled our feet behind
    them,
and pulled our heads.
We never knew the war, standing so small
looking at eye-level toward the puttees, searching
the picture-books for sceptres, pennants for truth;
see Galahad unaided by puberty.

Ratat a drum upon the armistice,
Kodak As You Go   :   photo   :   they danced late,
and we were a generation of grim children
leaning over the bedroom sills, watching
the music and the shoulders and how the war was
        over,
laughing until the blow on the mouth broke night
wide out from cover.
The child's curls blow in a forgotten wind,
immortal ivy trembles on the wall:
the sun has crystallized these scenes, and tall
shadows remember time cannot rescind.

III

Organize the full results of that rich past
open the windows   :   potent catalyst,
harsh theory of knowledge, running down the aisles
crying out in the classrooms, March ravening on the
        plain,
inexorable sun and wind and natural thought.
Dialectically our youth unfolds   :
the pale child walking to the river, passional
in ignorance   in loneliness   demanding
its habitation for the leaping dream, kissing
quick air, the vibrations of transient light,
not knowing substance or reserve, walking
in valvular air, each person in the street
conceived surrounded by his life and pain,
fixed against time, subtly by these impaled   :
death and that shapeless war.   Listening at dead doors,
our youth assumes a thousand differing flesh

summoning fact from abandoned machines of trade,
knocking on the wall of the nailed-up power-plant,
telephoning hello, the deserted factory, ready
for the affirmative clap of truth
ricochetting from thought to thought among
the childhood, the gestures, the rigid travellers.

Effort at Speech Between Two People

: Speak to me.   Take my hand.   What are you now?
I will tell you all.   I will conceal nothing.
When I was three, a little child read a story about a
     rabbit
who died, in the story, and I crawled under a chair   :
a pink rabbit   :   it was my birthday, and a candle
burnt a sore spot on my finger, and I was told to be
     happy.

: Oh, grow to know me.   I am not happy.   I will be
     open:
Now I am thinking of white sails against a sky like
     music,
like glad horns blowing, and birds tilting, and an arm
     about me.
There was one I loved, who wanted to live, sailing.

: Speak to me.   Take my hand.   What are you now?
When I was nine, I was fruitily sentimental,
fluid   :   and my widowed aunt played Chopin,

and I bent my head on the painted woodwork, and
   wept.
I want now to be close to you.   I would
link the minutes of my days close, somehow, to your
   days.

:   I am not happy.   I will be open.
I have liked lamps in evening corners, and quiet
   poems.
There has been fear in my life.   Sometimes I
   speculate
On what a tragedy his life was, really.

:   Take my hand.   Fist my mind in your hand.   What
   are you now?
When I was fourteen, I had dreams of suicide,
and I stood at a steep window, at sunset, hoping
   toward death   :
if the light had not melted clouds and plains to
   beauty,
if light had not transformed that day, I would have
   leapt.
I am unhappy.   I am lonely.   Speak to me.

:   I will be open.   I think he never loved me:
he loved the bright beaches, the little lips of foam
that ride small waves, he loved the veer of gulls:
he said with a gay mouth: I love you.   Grow to
   know me.

: What are you now?   If we could touch one another,
   if these our separate entities could come to grips,
   clenched like a Chinese puzzle . . . yesterday
   I stood in a crowded street that was live with people,
   and no one spoke a word, and the morning shone.
   Everyone silent, moving. . . . Take my hand.
        Speak to me.

Notes for a Poem

Here are the long fields inviolate of thought,
here are the planted fields raking the sky,
signs in the earth   :
water-cast shuttles of light flickering the underside of
     rock.
These have been shown before; but the fields know new
     hands,
the son's fingers grasp warmly at the father's hoe   ;
there will be new ways of seeing these ancestral lands.

     "In town, the munitions plant has been poor since
          the war,
     And nothing but a war will make it rich again."
     Holy, holy, holy, sings the church next door.

Time-ridden, a man strides the current of a stream's
     flowing,
stands, flexing the wand curvingly over his head,
tracking the water's prism with the flung line.

Summer becomes productive and mature.
Farmers watch tools like spikes of doom against the sure
condemning sky descending upon the hollow lands.

The water is ridged in muscles on the rock,
force for the State is planted in the stream-bed.
Water springs from the stone　——　the State is fed.

Morning comes, brisk with light,
a broom of color over the threshold.
Long flights of shadows escape to the white sky　:
a spoon is straightened.　　Day grows.　　The sky is
　　blued.

The water rushes over the shelves of stone
to anti-climax on the mills below the drop.
The planted fields are bright and rake the sky.
Power is common.　　Earth is grown
and overgrown in unrelated strength, the moral
rehearsed already, often.
(There must be the gearing of these facts
into coördination, in a poem or numbers,
rows of statistics, or the cool iambs.)
The locked relationships which will be found
are a design to build these factual timbers—
a plough of thought to break this stubborn ground.

Sand-Quarry with Moving Figures

Father and I drove to the sand-quarry across the ruined
    marshlands,
miles of black grass, burned for next summer's green.
I reached my hand to his beneath the lap-robe,
we looked at the stripe of fire, the blasted scene.

"It's all right," he said, "they can control the flames,
on one side men are standing, and on the other the sea;"
but I was terrified of stubble and waste of black
and his ugly villages he built and was showing me.

The countryside turned right and left about the car,
straight through October we drove to the pit's heart;
sand, and its yellow canyon and standing pools
and the wealth of the split country set us farther apart.
"Look," he said, "this quarry means rows of little
    houses,
stucco and a new bracelet for you are buried there;"
but I remembered the ruined patches, and I saw the land
    ruined,
exploded, burned away, and the fiery marshes bare.

"We'll own the countryside, you'll see how soon I will,
you'll have acres to play in"   :   I saw the written name
painted on stone in the face of the steep hill:
"That's your name, Father!"   "And yours!" he shouted,
    laughing.
"No, Father, no!"   He caught my hand as I cried,
and smiling, entered the pit, ran laughing down its side.

Three Sides of a Coin

I

Am I in your light?
No, go on reading
(the hackneyed light of evening quarrelling with
the bulbs;
the book's bent rectangle solid on your knees)
only my fingers in your hair, only, my eyes
splitting the skull to tickle your brain with love
in a slow caress blurring the mind,
kissing your mouth awake
opening the body's mouth and stopping the words.
This light is thick with birds, and
evening warns us beautifully of death.
Slowly I bend over you, slowly your breath
runs rhythms through my blood
as if I said
I love you
and you should raise your head
listening, speaking into the covert night
:   Did someone say something?
Love, am I in your light?
Am I?

Refrain   See how love alters the living face
go spin the immortal coin through time
watch the thing flip through space
tick   tick

We all had a good time
                    the throne was there and all
and there she was with that primitive unforgivable
    mouth
saying sophistications about nothing at all
as the young men cavorted up the room Darling
it's a swell party and those Martinis with
the olives so delicately soaked in alcohol
    and William Flesh, the inventor, being cute
about the revolution and the Negro Question
until Dick said "Lynch the Jews!" (his name was
    Fleischman
but the war brought about a number of changes)
and the Objectivist poet fresh from Butte
with his prePosterous suggestion. . . .
    After a while, of course, we left,
the room was getting so jammed with editors.
And William and Maurice and Del and I
went back and we took turns using the couch with them.
    We all had a good time,
and Del had hysterics at about 3 a.m.
    we dashed water into her face
    I held her temples and Maurice said
    what could we hope to look for next:
    it's one thing to be faithful to the dead
    (he said) but for her to stick to an oversexed
old fool : but she only laughed and cried and beat
    the floor
until the neighbors rattled at the door.

Refrain   Runnels of wine ran down his chin and laughter
          softened his words until quite suddenly
          the walls fell and the night stood blank and
               after
                    tick   tick

     III

He turned the lights on and walked to the window   :
Son of a bitch   :   he said   :   if it isn't the reds again
parading through the streets with those lousy posters.
The Village was never like this in the old days,
throw a brick down the street and you'd hit a female
     poet
and life went on like a string of roller coasters.

                    Workers of the world   :
we've worked the world for all the damn thing's worth
                    tick   tick
I was little and they promised me the hills of glory
a great life and a sounding name on the earth   :
                    tick   tick
               this is a different story.

Here's a list I've been making   :   reasons for living
on the right, reasons for my sudden death on the left.
Right now they balance so I could flip a coin
determine the imperative tonight
                    tick   tick
flip that amazing coin through time and space this night
and the Village   :   and the army with banners
                         and the hot girls

and the rotgut all gone
                              like a blown fuse   :
I'd get a paragraph or two of news
obituary as a shutting door
meaning no more
leaving the world to the sun and the workers
the straight beautiful children   the coins   the clocks
                              tick   tick

This House, This Country

Always I travelled farther
dreading a barrier
starting at shadows scattered on the ground
fearful of the invisible night-sound,

till in that straight career
I crossed frontier
the questions asked   the proofs shown   the name
signed smiling   I reached knowledge of my home.

I praised their matings
and corner-meetings
their streets the brightest I had yet walked down   :
my family swore I did not leave my town

thought that I lied
and had not signed
those passports, tickets, contracts, bills of sale
but still rested among them and wished them well.

Over my shoulder
I see they grow older
their vision fails   :   observe I travel light
fear distance   hope I shall only spend the night.

But night in this country
is deep promise of day,
is busy with preparations and awake for fighting
and there is no time for leavetaking and regretting.

I know their tired house
full of remorse
I know in my body the door, the entrance-hall
a wall and my space and another wall.

I have left forever
house and maternal river
given up sitting in that private tomb
quitted that land   that house   that velvet room.

Frontiers admitted me
to a growing country
I carry the proofs of my birth and my mind's reasons
but reckon with their struggle and their seasons.

The Structure of the Plane

I. The Structure of the Plane

Kitty Hawk is a Caesar among monuments   ;
      the stiff bland soldiers predestined to their death
      the bombs piled neatly like children's marbles piled
      sperm to breed corpses eugenically by youth
      out of seductive death.
                        The hill outdoes our towers
      we might treasure a thistle grown from a cannon-
          mouth
      they have not permitted rust and scum and
          blossoms
      to dirty the steel,
                however we have the plane
the hill, flower among monuments.

"To work intelligently" (Orville and Wilbur Wright)
"one needs to know the effects of variations
incorporated in the surfaces. . . . The pressures on
      squares
are different from those on rectangles, circles, triangles,
      or ellipses . . .
The shape of the edge also makes a difference."

The plane is wheeled out of the hangar.   The sleeves
      shake
fixing the wind, the four o'clock blue sky
blinks in the goggles swinging over his wrist.
The plane rests, the mechanic in cream-colored overalls

encourages the engine into idling speed.
The instructor looks at his class
and begins the demonstration.

"We finally became discouraged, and returned to kite-
        flying.
But as we grew older we had to give up this sport,
it was unbecoming to boys of our ages."

On the first stroke of the piston the intake valve opens,
the piston moves slowly from the head of the cylinder,
drawing in its mixture of gas and air.   On the second
        stroke
the piston returns, the valve closes.   The mixture is
        compressed.
A spark occurs, igniting America, opening India,
finding the Northwest Passage, Cipango spice,
causing the mixture to burn, expanding the gases
which push the piston away on the power stroke.
The final exhaust stroke serves to release the gases,
allowing the piston to scavenge the cylinder.
                We burn space, we sever galaxies,
                solar systems whirl about Shelley's head,
                we give ourselves ease, gentlemen, art and
                        these explosions
                and Peter Ronsard finger-deep in roses   ;
gentlemen, remember these incandescent points,
remember to check, remember to drain the oil,
remember Plato O remember me
                the college pathways rise
                the president's voice intoning sonnets

the impress of hoofmarks on the bridle path
the shining girls the lost virginities
the plane over a skeletal water-tower
our youth dissolving O remember
romantically dissolving remember me.

Blue smoke from the exhaust signifies too much oil.
Save yourselves from excesses, dirt, and tailspins.
These are the axioms   :   stability, control,
and equilibrium   :   in a yaw, in a roll, or pitch.
Here, gentlemen, are the wings, of fabric doped and
        painted
here is the rudder
here the propeller spins
:   BE   hammers in the brain
FLY and the footbeat of that drum
may not be contradicted
must be mine
must be made ours, say the brothers Wright together
        although the general public had been invited
        few dared a cold December
        in order to see another plane not fly.

The helmet is strapped tight, orders are shouted
the elbows of steel move in oil
air is forced under the ship, the pilot's hand
is safe on the stick, the young student sits
with the wind mottling his eyelashes, rigidly.
Centuries fall behind his brain, the motor
pushes in a four-beat rhythm, his blood moves,
he dares look at the levels mounting in clouds

the dropping fields of the sky the diminishment of
    earth   ;
         now he thinks I am the child crying Mother
         this rim is the threshold into the hall's night
         or the windowsill livened with narcissus.
         The white edge of the bath a moment before
         slipping into watery ease, the windowsill
         eager for the jump into the street
         the hard stone under my back, the earth
         with its eyes and hands its eyes and hands
         its eyes
             fixed eyes on the diminishing
         take me back the bath had fronds of steam
         escaping the hands held my head
         my eyes slipped in oil looking along your
            beauty
         earth is painful the distance hurts
         mother the night, the distance, dear
he is standing with one look of hate upon him
screams at the pilot you bastard, you bastard, jumps
trailing a long scream above him, the plane yaws down,
the motor pulls heavily, the ground is dark November,
his parachute opens a bright plume surrendering
    downward,
the plane heads up again, no good in following,
continues unfascinated by night or land or death.

    II. The Strike

"Well," he said, "George, I never thought you were with
    us.

You walked out of the shaft as if you'd spent years of
        your life
planning some day to walk out once without blinking
and not stop for a smoke but walk over to our side."

"No," he said, "I never expected to.   It was only the
        last cut:
before that, I'd have worked no matter who starved
        first."
The snow was stamped down with black nailprints
the stamping was a drum to warm them, stiff veins,
        crusted hands.

"Carrying guns, boys!" said the director.   "Now boys;
I'll speak to the others and see what I can do."
The heavy-set miner spat on the peel of snow.
The fingers weighed on the triggers.   December bit
into the bone, into the tight skulls, creaking one word.

Tell how the men watched the table, a plate of light,
the rigid faces lit around it, the mouths
opening and clamping, the little warmth
watched against the shafts of the breakers.
Tell how the men watched.
Tell how the child chewed its shoe to strips.

That day broke equal grey, the lockers empty,
the cages hanging in a depth of silence.
Shall we say   :   there were two lines at last   :
death played like a current between them, playing,
the little flames of death ran along those eyes   :   ?

Death faced the men with a desperate seduction,
lifted a hand with the skill of a hypnotist.
They were so ready in khaki with bayonets.

      "George!" he heard.   That had once been his
         name.
      Very carefully he had stepped from his place,
      walked over his ground, over the last line.
      It seemed impossible he should not die.

            When a gun faces you, look down
               the bore,
            that is the well of death :   when it
               confronts you
            it is not satisfied, it draws you
               steadily
            more loving than love, eagerer than
               hunger,
            resolving all unbalance.   He went
               to it.

However, the line held.   The plump men raised
      themselves
up from the chairs in a dreary passion of wrath,
hoisted themselves to the doorway.   Spoke.
There was his body, purpled, death casing him
in ice and velvet and sleep.   Indeed, they spoke,
this was unwarranted.   No, they conceded.   No.
Perhaps the strike might equal victory,
a company funeral, and the trucks of coal
               ladled up from the earth,
               heaped on this grave.

III. The Lover

Answer with me these certainties
of glands swelling with sentiment
the loves embittered the salts and waters mixing
a chemic threatening destruction.

Answer the men walking toward death
leaping to death meeting death in a kiss
able to find of equilibrium none
except that last of hard stone kissing stone.

Answer the lover's questioning in the streets
the evenings domed with purple, the bones
easing, the flesh slipping perfume upon the air   :
all surfaces of flight are pared to planes

equal, equilibrated, solid in fulfilment.   No way
is wanted to escape, no explosions craved,
only this desire must be met, this motion
be balanced with passion   ;

> in the wreaths of time given to us what love
> may reach us in the streets   the books   the
>   years
> what wreaths of love may touch our dreams,
> what skeins of fine response may clothe our
>   flesh,
> robe us in valor brave as our dear wish

lover haunting the ghosts of rivers, letting
    time
slide a fluid runner into darkness
give over the sad eyes the marble face of pain
do not mourn : remember : do not
    forget
but never let this treason play you mate,

take to yourself the branches of green trees
watch the clean sky signed by the flight of
    planes
know rivers of love   be flooded thoroughly
by love and the years and the past and know
the green tree perishes and green trees grow.

Knock at the doors ; go to the windows ; run,
you will not find her soon who, lost in love,
relinquished last month to that silver music
repeating in her throat forsaken tunes.

Rigid and poised for the latest of these lovers
she stretches acute in waiting on the bed
most avaricious for the length of arms
the subtle thighs and heavy confident head.

Taut with a steel strut's singing tautness she
clinches her softness anguished at postponement
hardening all her thought she swears to be
unpacified by minutes of atonement.

The ticking of an ormolu clock taxes
her body with time's weight.   The opened door
adjusts such things   ;   responsive, she relaxes
ringing in answer to a word before

all tensity is changed to eagerness.
Translated and resolved, the anguish through,
sensitive altogether to the present   :
"Now?"   "Yes," she says, "yes," she says, "do."

———

Answer motion with motion, be birds flying
be the enormous movements of the snows,
be rain, be love, remain equilibrated
unseeking death,
                    if you must have pilgrimages
go travelling to balance need with answer
suiting the explosion to the ensuing shock
the foil to the airstream running over it
food to the mouth, tools to the body, mind
to the bright mind that leaps in necessity
go answering   answering   FLY

Study in a Late Subway

The moon revolves outside; possibly, black air
turns so around them facing night's concave,
momentum the slogan of their hurling brains
swung into speed, crying for stillness   high
     suspended and rising on time's wave.

Did these tracks have a wilder life in the ground?
beaten from streams of metal in secret earth   :
energy travels along the veins of steel,
their faces rush forward, missiles of discontent
        thrown vaguely to the south and north.

That head is jointed loosely on his neck,
his glossy eyes turn on the walls and floor   :
her face is a blank breast with sorrow
spouting at the mouth's nipple.   All eyes move
        heavily to the opening door,

regarding in dullness how we also enter.
An angle of track charges up to us, swings
out and past in a firework of signals.
Sleepily others dangle by one hand
        tense and semi-crucified things.

Speed welcomes us in explosions of night   :   here
is wrath and fortitude and motion's burning   :
the world buries the directionless, until
the heads are sprung in awareness or drowned in peace.
        Sleep will happen.   We must give them morning.

FROM **The Book of the Dead**

THE ROAD

These are roads to take when you think of your country
and interested bring down the maps again,
phoning the statistician, asking the dear friend,

reading the papers with morning inquiry.
Or when you sit at the wheel and your small light
chooses gas gauge and clock; and the headlights

indicate future of road, your wish pursuing
past the junction, the fork, the suburban station,
well-travelled six-lane highway planned for safety.

Past your tall central city's influence,
outside its body: traffic, penumbral crowds,
are centers removed and strong, fighting for good
    reason.

These roads will take you into your own country.
Select the mountains, follow rivers back,
travel the passes. Touch West Virginia where

the Midland Trail leaves the Virginia furnace,
iron Clifton Forge, Covington iron, goes down
into the wealthy valley, resorts, the chalk hotel.

Pillars and fairway; spa; White Sulphur Springs.
Airport. Gay blank rich faces wishing to add
history to ballrooms, tradition to the first tee.

The simple mountains, sheer, dark-graded with pine
in the sudden weather, wet outbreak of spring,
crosscut by snow, wind at the hill's shoulder.

The land is fierce here, steep, braced against snow,
rivers and spring. KING COAL HOTEL, Lookout,
and swinging the vicious bend, New River Gorge.

Now the photographer unpacks camera and case,
surveying the deep country, follows discovery
viewing on groundglass an inverted image.

John Marshall named the rock (steep pines, a drop
he reckoned in 1812, called) Marshall's Pillar,
but later, Hawk's Nest. Here is your road, tying

you to its meanings: gorge, boulder, precipice.
Telescoped down, the hard and stone-green river
cutting fast and direct into the town.

STATEMENT: PHILIPPA ALLEN

—You like the State of West Virginia very much, do you
   not?
—I do very much, in the summertime.
—How much time have you spent in West Virginia?
—During the summer of 1934, when I was doing social
   work down there, I first heard of what we were
   pleased to call the Gauley tunnel tragedy, which in-
   volved about 2,000 men.
—What was their salary?
—It started at 40¢ and dropped to 25¢ an hour.
—You have met these people personally?
—I have talked to people; yes.
   According to estimates of contractors
   2,000 men were
            employed there
            period, about 2 years
            drilling, 3.75 miles of tunnel.
            To divert water (from New River)
            to a hydroelectric plant (at Gauley Junction).
   The rock through which they were boring was of a
      high silica content.
   In tunnel No. 1 it ran 97–99% pure silica.
   The contractors
            knowing pure silica
            30 years' experience
            must have known danger for every man
   neglected to provide the workmen with any safety
      device. . . .

—As a matter of fact, they originally intended to dig
that tunnel a certain size?

—Yes.

—And then enlarged the size of the tunnel, due to the
fact that they discovered silica and wanted to get it
out?

—That is true for tunnel No. 1.

   The tunnel is part of a huge water-power project
         begun, latter part of 1929
         direction: New Kanawha Power Co.
             subsidiary of Union Carbide &
              Carbon Co.
         That company—licensed:
         to develop power for public sale.
         Ostensibly it was to do that; but
         (in reality) it was formed to sell all the power to
             the Electro-Metallurgical Co.
             subsidiary of Union Carbide &
              Carbon Co.
               which by an act of the State
                legislature
             was allowed to buy up
             New Kanawha Power Co. in 1933.

—They were developing the power. What I am trying
to get at, Miss Allen, is, did they use this silica from
the tunnel; did they afterward sell it and use it in
commerce?

—They used it in the electro-processing of steel.

  SiO_2 SiO_2

  The richest deposit.

Shipped on the C & O down to Alloy.
It was so pure that
$$SiO_2$$
they used it without refining.
—Where did you stay?
—I stayed at Cedar Grove. Some days I would have to
    hitch into Charleston, other days to Gauley Bridge.
—You found the people of West Virginia very happy to
    pick you up on the highway, did you not?
—Yes; they are delightfully obliging.
  (All were bewildered. Again at Vanetta they are
        asking, "What can be done about this?")
  I feel that this investigation may help in some
    manner.
  I do hope it may.
  I am now making a very general statement as a
    beginning. There are many points that I should
    like to develop later, but I shall try to give you a
    general history of this condition first. . . .

GAULEY BRIDGE

Camera at the crossing sees the city
a street of wooden walls and empty windows,
the doors shut handless in the empty street,
and the deserted Negro standing on the corner.

The little boy runs with his dog
up the street to the bridge over the river where
nine men are mending road for the government.
He blurs the camera-glass fixed on the street.

Railway tracks here and many panes of glass
tin under light, the grey shine of towns and forests:
in the commercial hotel (Switzerland of America)
the owner is keeping his books behind the public glass.

Postoffice window, a hive of private boxes,
the hand of the man who withdraws, the woman who
        reaches her hand
and the tall coughing man stamping an envelope.

The bus station and the great pale buses stopping for
        food;
April-glass-tinted, the yellow-aproned waitress;
coast-to-coast schedule on the plateglass window.

The man on the street and the camera eye:
he leaves the doctor's office, slammed door, doom,
any town looks like this one-street town.

Glass, wood, and naked eye: the movie-house
closed for the afternoon frames posters streaked with
        rain,
advertise "Racing Luck" and "Hitch-Hike Lady."

Whistling, the train comes from a long way away,
slow, and the Negro watches it grow in the grey air,
the hotel man makes a note behind his potted palm.

Eyes of the tourist house, red-and-white filling station,
the eyes of the Negro, looking down the track,
hotel-man and hotel, cafeteria, camera.

And in the beerplace on the other sidewalk
always one's harsh night eyes over the beerglass
follow the waitress and the yellow apron.

The road flows over the bridge,
Gamoca pointer at the underpass,
opposite, Alloy, after a block of town.

What do you want—a cliff over a city?
A foreland, sloped to sea and overgrown with roses?
These people live here.

THE DISEASE

This is a lung disease. Silicate dust makes it.
The dust causing the growth of

This is the X-ray picture taken last April.
I would point out to you: these are the ribs;
this is the region of the breastbone;
this is the heart (a wide white shadow filled with blood).
In here of course is the swallowing tube, esophagus.
The windpipe. Spaces between the lungs.

Between the ribs?

Between the ribs. These are the collar bones.
Now, this lung's mottled, beginning, in these areas.
You'd say a snowstorm had struck the fellow's lungs.
About alike, that side and this side, top and bottom.
The first stage in this period in this case.

Let us have the second.

Come to the window again. Here is the heart.
More numerous nodules, thicker, see, in the upper
  lobes.
You will notice the increase   :   here, streaked fibrous
  tissue—

Indicating?

That indicates the progress in ten months' time.
And now, this year—short breathing, solid scars
even over the ribs, thick on both sides.
Blood vessels shut. Model conglomeration.

What stage?

Third stage. Each time I place my pencil point:
There and there and there, there, there.

"It is growing worse every day. At night
"I get up to catch my breath. If I remained
"flat on my back I believe I would die."

It gradually chokes off the air cells in the lungs?
I am trying to say it the best I can.
That is what happens, isn't it?
A choking-off in the air cells?

Yes.
>   There is difficulty in breathing.
Yes.
>   And a painful cough?
Yes.

>   Does silicosis cause death?

Yes, sir.

THE CORNFIELD

Error, disease, snow, sudden weather.
For those given to contemplation :   this house,
wading in snow, its cracks are sealed with clay,
walls papered with print, newsprint repeating,
in-focus grey across the room, and squared
ads for a book :   HEAVEN'S MY DESTINATION,
HEAVEN'S MY . . . HEAVEN. . . . THORNTON WILDER.
The long-faced man rises long-handed jams the door
tight against snow, long-boned, he shivers.
Contemplate.

>   Swear by the corn,
the found-land corn, those who like ritual. *He*
rides in a good car. They say blind corpses rode
with him in front, knees broken into angles,
head clamped ahead. Overalls. Affidavits.
He signs all papers. His office :   where he sits,

feet on the stove, loaded trestles through door,
satin-lined, silk-lined, unlined, cheap.
The papers in the drawer. On the desk, photograph
H. C. White, Funeral Services (new car and eldest son);
tells about Negroes who got wet at work,
shot craps, drank and took cold, pneumonia, died.
Shows the sworn papers. Swear by the corn.
Pneumonia, pneumonia, pleurisy, t.b.

For those given to voyages   :   these roads
discover gullies, invade, Where does it go now?
Now turn upstream twenty-five yards. Now road again.
Ask the man on the road. Saying, That cornfield?
Over the second hill, through the gate,
watch for the dogs. Buried, five at a time,
pine boxes, Rinehart & Dennis paid him $55
a head for burying these men in plain pine boxes.
His mother is suing him   :   misuse of land.
George Robinson   :   I knew a man
who died at four in the morning at the camp.
At seven his wife took clothes to dress her dead
husband, and at the undertaker's
they told her the husband was already buried.
—Tell me this, the men with whom you are acquainted,
the men who have this disease
have been told that sooner or later they are going to
        die?
—Yes, sir.
—How does that seem to affect the majority of the
        people?
—It don't work on anything but their wind.

—Do they seem to be living in fear
or do they wish to die?
—They are getting to breathe a little faster.

For those given to keeping their own garden:
Here is the cornfield, white and wired by thorns,
old cornstalks, snow, the planted home.
Stands bare against a line of farther field,
unmarked except for wood stakes, charred at tip,
few scratched and named (pencil or nail).
Washed-off. Under the mounds,
all the anonymous.
Abel America, calling from under the corn,
Earth, uncover my blood!
Did the undertaker know the man was married?
Uncover.
Do they seem to fear death?
Contemplate.
Does Mellon's ghost walk, povertied at last,
walking in furrows of corn, still sowing,
do apparitions come?
Voyage.
Think of your gardens. But here is corn to keep.
Marked pointed sticks to name the crop beneath.
Sowing is over, harvest is coming ripe.

—No, sir; they want to go on.
They want to live as long as they can.

THE DAM

All power is saved, having no end.   Rises
in the green season, in the sudden season
the white the budded

                      and the lost.
Water celebrates, yielding continually
sheeted and fast in its overfall
slips down the rock, evades the pillars
building its colonnades, repairs
in stream and standing wave
retains its seaward green
broken by obstacle rock; falling, the water sheet
spouts, and the mind dances, excess of white.
White brilliant function of the land's disease.

Many-spanned, lighted, the crest leans under
concrete arches and the channelled hills,
turns in the gorge toward its release;
kinetic and controlled, the sluice
urging the hollow, the thunder,
the major climax

                      energy
total and open watercourse
praising the spillway, fiery glaze,
crackle of light, cleanest velocity
flooding, the moulded force.

> *I open out a way over the water*
> *I form a path between the Combatants:*
> *Grant that I sail down like a living bird,*
> *power over the fields and Pool of Fire.*
> *Phoenix, I sail over the phoenix world.*

Diverted water, the fern and fuming white
ascend in mist of continuous diffusion.
Rivers are turning inside their mountains,
streams line the stone, rest at the overflow
lake and in lanes of pliant color lie.
Blessing of this innumerable silver,
printed in silver, images of stone
walk on a screen of falling water
in film-silver in continual change
recurring colored, plunging with the wave.

Constellations of light, abundance of many rivers.
The sheeted island-cities, the white surf filling west,
the hope, fast water spilled where still pools fed.
Great power flying deep: between the rock and the
        sunset,
the caretaker's house and the steep abutment,
hypnotic water fallen and the tunnels under
the moist and fragile galleries of stone,
mile-long, under the wave. Whether snow fall,
the quick light fall, years of white cities fall,
flood that this valley built falls slipping down
the green turn in the river's green.
Steep gorge, the wedge of crystal in the sky.

How many feet of whirlpools?
What is a year in terms of falling water?
Cylinders; kilowatts; capacities.
Continuity: $\Sigma\, Q = 0$
Equations for falling water. The streaming motion.
The balance-sheet of energy that flows
passing along its infinite barrier.

It breaks the hills, cracking the riches wide,
runs through electric wires;
it comes, warning the night,
running among these rigid hills,
a single force to waken our eyes.

They poured the concrete and the columns stood,
laid bare the bedrock, set the cells of steel,
a dam for monument was what they hammered home.
Blasted, and stocks went up;
insured the base,
and limousines
wrote their own graphs upon
roadbed and lifeline.

Their hands touched mastery:
wait for defense, solid across the world.
Mr. Griswold. "A corporation is a body without a soul."
Mr. Dunn. When they were caught at it they resorted to
the methods employed by gunmen, ordinary ma-
chine gun racketeers. They cowardly tried to buy
out the people who had the information on them.
Mr. Marcantonio. I agree that a racket has been prac-
tised, but the most damnable racketeering that I
have ever known is the paying of a fee to the very
attorney who represented these victims. That is the
most outrageous racket that has ever come within
my knowledge.
Miss Allen. Mr. Jesse J. Ricks, the president of the
Union Carbide & Carbon Corporation, suggested
that the stockholder had better take this question
up in a private conference.

The dam is safe. A scene of power.
The dam is the father of the tunnel.
This is the valley's work, the white, the shining.

High	Low	Stock and Dividend in Dollars	Open	High	Low	Last	Net Chge.	Closing		
								Bid	Ask	Sales
111	61¼	Union Carbide (3.20)	67¼	69½	67¼	69½	+3	69¼	69½	3,400

The dam is used when the tunnel is used.
The men and the water are never idle,
have definitions.
This is a perfect fluid, having no age nor hours,
surviving scarless, unaltered, loving rest,
willing to run forever to find its peace
in equal seas in currents of still glass.
Effects of friction : to fight and pass again,
learning its power, conquering boundaries,
able to rise blind in revolts of tide,
broken and sacrificed to flow resumed.
Collecting eternally power. Spender of power,
torn, never can be killed, speeded in filaments,
million, its power can rest and rise forever,
wait and be flexible. Be born again.
Nothing is lost, even among the wars,
imperfect flow, confusion of force.
It will rise. These are the phases of its face.
It knows its seasons, the waiting, the sudden.
It changes. It does not die.

THE BOOK OF THE DEAD

These roads will take you into your own country.
Seasons and maps coming where this road comes
into a landscape mirrored in these men.

Past all your influences, your home river,
constellations of cities, mottoes of childhood,
parents and easy cures, war, all evasion's wishes.

What one word must never be said?
Dead, and these men fight off our dying,
cough in the theatres of the war.

What two things shall never be seen?
They : what we did.   Enemy : what we mean.
This is a nation's scene and halfway house.

What three things can never be done?
Forget.   Keep silent.   Stand alone.
The hills of glass, the fatal brilliant plain.

The facts of war forced into actual grace.
Seasons and modern glory.   Told in the histories,
                    how first ships came

seeing on the Atlantic thirteen clouds
lining the west horizon with their white
                    shining halations;

they conquered, throwing off impossible Europe—
could not be used to transform; created coast—
            breathed-in America.

See how they took the land, made after-life
fresh out of exile, planted the pioneer
            base and blockade,

pushed forests down in an implacable walk
west where new clouds lay at the desirable
            body of sunset;

taking the seaboard.   Replaced the isolation,
dropped cities where they stood, drew a tidewater
            frontier of Europe,

a moment, and another frontier held,
this land was planted home-land that we know.
            Ridge of discovery,

until we walk to windows, seeing America
lie in a photograph of power, widened
            before our forehead,

and still behind us falls another glory,
London unshaken, the long French road to Spain,
            the old Mediterranean

flashing new signals from the hero hills
near Barcelona, monuments and powers,
            parent defenses.

Before our face the broad and concrete west,
green ripened field, frontier pushed back like river
        controlled and dammed;

the flashing wheatfields, cities, lunar plains
grey in Nevada, the sane fantastic country
        sharp in the south,

liveoak, the hanging moss, a world of desert,
the dead, the lava, and the extreme arisen
        fountains of life,

the flourished land, peopled with watercourses
to California and the colored sea;
        sums of frontiers

and unmade boundaries of acts and poems,
the brilliant scene between the seas, and standing,
        this fact and this disease.

———

Half-memories absorb us, and our ritual world
carries its history in familiar eyes,
planted in flesh it signifies its music

in minds which turn to sleep and memory,
in music knowing all the shimmering names,
the spear, the castle, and the rose.

But planted in our flesh these valleys stand,
everywhere we begin to know the illness,
are forced up, and our times confirm us all.

In the museum life, centuries of ambition
yielded at last a fertilizing image:
the Carthaginian stone meaning a tall woman

carries in her two hands the book and cradled dove,
on her two thighs, wings folded from the waist
cross to her feet, a pointed human crown.

This valley is given to us like a glory.
To friends in the old world, and their lifting hands
that call for intercession. Blow falling full in face.

All those whose childhood made learn skill to meet,
and art to see after the change of heart;
all the belligerents who know the world.

You standing over gorges, surveyors and planners,
you workers and hope of countries, first among powers;
you who give peace and bodily repose,

opening landscapes by grace, giving the marvel lowlands
physical peace, flooding old battlefields
with general brilliance, who best love your lives;

and you young, you who finishing the poem
wish new perfection and begin to make;
you men of fact, measure our times again.

———

These are our strength, who strike against history.
These whose corrupt cells owe their new styles of
        weakness
                to our diseases;

these carrying light for safety on their foreheads
descended deeper for richer faults of ore,
                drilling their death.

These touching radium and the luminous poison,
carried their death on their lips and with their warning
                glow in their graves.

These weave and their eyes water and rust away,
these stand at wheels until their brains corrode,
                these farm and starve,

all these men cry their doom across the world,
meeting avoidable death, fight against madness,
                find every war.

Are known as strikers, soldiers, pioneers,
fight on all new frontiers, are set in solid
                lines of defense.

Defense is sight; widen the lens and see
standing over the land myths of identity,
                new signals, processes:

Alloys begin   :   certain dominant metals.
Deliberate combines add new qualities,
                    sums of new uses.

Over the country, from islands of Maine fading,
Cape Sable fading south into the orange
                    detail of sunset,

new processes, new signals, new possession.
A name for all the conquests, prediction of victory
                    deep in these powers.

Carry abroad the urgent need, the scene,
to photograph and to extend the voice,
                    to speak this meaning.

Voices to speak to us directly.   As we move.
As we enrich, growing in larger motion,
                    this word, this power.

Down coasts of taken countries, mastery,
discovery at one hand, and at the other
                    frontiers and forests,

fanatic cruel legend at our back and
speeding ahead the red and open west,
                    and this our region,

desire, field, beginning.   Name and road,
communication to these many men,
as epilogue, seeds of unending love.

Girl at the Play

Long after you beat down the powerful hand
and leave the scene, prison's still there to break.
Brutalized by escape, you travel out to sit
in empty theatres, your stunned breast, hardened neck
            waiting for warmth to venture back.

Gilded above the stage, staring archaic shapes
hang, like those men you learn submission from
whose majesty sits yellow on the night,
young indolent girls, long-handed, one's vague mouth
            and cruel nose and jaw and throat.

Waiting's paralysis strikes, king-cobra hooded head's
infected fangs petrify body and face.
Emblems fade everyway, dissolving even
the bitter infantile boys who call for sleep's
            winy breasts whose nipples are long
            grapes.

Seats fill. The curtain's up where strong lights act,
cut theatre to its theme; the quick fit's past.
Here's answer in masses moving; by light elect,
they turn the stage before into the street behind;
            and nothing's so forgotten as your blind
            female paralysis that takes the mind,
            and nothing's so forgotten as your dead
            fever, now that it's past and the swift play's
            ahead.

Homage to Literature

When you imagine trumpet-faced musicians
blowing again inimitable jazz
no art can accuse nor cannonadings hurt,

or coming out of your dreams of dirigibles
again see thc unreasonable cripple
throwing his crutch headlong as the headlights

streak down the torn street, as the three hammerers
go One, Two, Three on the stake, triphammer
        poundings
and not a sign of new worlds to still the heart;

then stare into the lake of sunset as it runs
boiling, over the west past all control
rolling and swamps the heartbeat and repeats
sea beyond sea after unbearable suns;
think: poems fixed this landscape: Blake, Donne, Keats.

More of a Corpse Than a Woman

Give them my regards when you go to the school
        reunion;
and at the marriage-supper, say that I'm thinking about
        them.
They'll remember my name; I went to the movies with
        that one,

feeling the weight of their death where she sat at my
    elbow;
                she never said a word,
                but all of them were heard.

All of them alike, expensive girls, the leaden friends:
one used to play the piano, one of them once wrote a
    sonnet,
one even seemed awakened enough to photograph
    wheatfields—
the dull girls with the educated minds and technical
    passions—
                pure love was their employment,
                they tried it for enjoyment.

Meet them at the boat   :   they've brought the
    souvenirs of boredom,
a seashell from the faltering monarchy;
the nose of a marble saint; and from the battlefield,
an empty shell divulged from a flower-bed.
                The lady's wealthy breath
                perfumes the air with death.

The leaden lady faces the fine, voluptuous woman,
faces a rising world bearing its gifts in its hands.
Kisses her casual dreams upon the lips she kisses,
risen, she moves away; takes others; moves away.
                Inadequate to love,
                supposes she's enough.

Give my regards to the well-protected woman,
I knew the ice-cream girl, we went to school together.
There's something to bury, people, when you begin to
bury.
When your women are ready and rich in their wish for
the world,
destroy the leaden heart,
we've a new race to start.

Woman and Emblems

Woman and Bird

A bird flew out of a cloud
(with a beak, flying),
broke its beak on my bone,
cried bird-cries over crying.

Sky, stranger, wilderness
(flying starry through flesh),
make an end; be me, bird.
It reverses my one wish.

Bird screams slavery among bones.
(I watch with a bird's eyes.)
Quarrel, wings; if I travel,
bird stays—stand, bird flies.

Bird sets feathers where flesh was
(my claws slide away on space).

Bird, here—now, bird, we fly!
Mourns, mourns, it turns a captive face.

The Birthday

A sound lying on the fantastic air
opens the night and the child is born;
as the wind moves, the solemn crying
pioneers in the air, changes

to flame crusading among the grasses
fire-whitened, aroused before it,
rippled crops—and blazing races
into a central arena

where it stands as a fighting-cock
conqueror head, aggressive spur,
and the gilt feather, the bronze, the greenish,
flicker and threaten.

The feathers of the fighting-cock
become a tree, and casting seed,
raise potent forests at its side—
birth among burning.

The great magnetic branches sign
meaning on the record sky—
now rise, moon, stiffen, bird, and flames,
kill and engender.

Reversal, chameleon,
pursuing images—
recurrent birth offering other names,
a spool of brightness.

Woman and Music

This is a tall woman walking through a square
thinking what is a woman at midnight in a park
under bells, in the trivial and lovely hours
with images, violins, dancers approaching?

This is a woman sitting at a mirror
her back to the glass and all the dancers advancing,
or in a chair laughing at a bone
sitting upright in a chair
talking of ballet, flesh's impermanence.

This is a woman looking at a stage—
dancer receiving the floral blue and white,
balanced against a tallest blue decor,
dancing—and all the parks, walks, hours
descend in brilliant water past the eyes
pursuing and forgotten and subdued
to blinding music, the deliberate strings.

First Elegy. Rotten Lake

As I went down to Rotten Lake I remembered
the wrecked season, haunted by plans of salvage,
snow, the closed door, footsteps and resurrections,
　　　machinery of sorrow.

The warm grass gave to the feet and the stilltide water
was floor of evening and magnetic light and
reflection of wish, the black-haired beast with my eyes
　　　walking beside me.

The green and yellow lights, the street of water
　　　standing
point to the image of that house whose destruction
I weep when I weep you.　My door (no), poems, rest,
　　　(don't say it!) untamable need.
　　　　　　───

When you have left the river you are a little way
nearer the lake; but I leave many times.
Parents parried my past; the present was poverty,
the future depended on my unfinished spirit.
There were no misgivings because there was no choice,
only regret for waste, and the wild knowledge:
growth and sorrow and discovery.

When you have left the river you proceed alone;
all love is likely to be illicit; and few
friends to command the soul; they are too feeble.
Rejecting the subtle and contemplative minds
as being too thin in the bone; and the gross thighs
and unevocative hands fail also.   But the poet
and his wife, those who say Survive, remain;
and those two who were with me on the ship
leading me to the sum of the years, in Spain.

When you have left the river you will hear the war.
In the mountains, with tourists, in the insanest groves
the sound of kill, the precious face of peace.
And the sad frightened child, continual minor,
returns, nearer whole circle, O and nearer
all that was loved, the lake, the naked river,
what must be crossed and cut out of your heart,
what must be stood beside and straightly seen.

———

As I went down to Rotten Lake I remembered
how the one crime is need.   The man lifting the loaf
with hunger as motive can offer no alibi, is
          always condemned.

These are the lines at the employment bureau
and the tense students at their examinations;
needing makes clumsy and robs them of their wish,
          in one fast gesture

plants on them failure of the imagination;
and lovers who lower their bodies into the chair

gently and sternly as if the flesh had been wounded,
        never can conquer.

Their need is too great, their vulnerable bodies
rigidly joined will snap, turn love away,
fear parts them, they lose their hands and voices, never
        get used to the world.

Walking at night, they are asked Are you your best
        friend's
best friend? and must say No, not yet, they are
love's vulnerable, and they go down to Rotten Lake
        hoping for wonders.

Dare it arrive, the day when weakness ends?
When the insistence is strong, the wish converted?
I prophesy the meeting by the water
        of these desires.

I know what this is, I have known the waking
when every night ended in one cliff-dream
of faces drowned beneath the porous rock
        brushed by the sea;

suffered the change   :   deprived erotic dreams
to images of that small house where peace
walked room to room and always with one face
        telling her stories,

and needed that, past loss, past fever, and the
attractive enemy who in my bed

touches all night the body of my sleep,
      improves my summer

with madness, impossible loss, and the dead music
of altered promise, a room torn up by the roots,
the desert that crosses from the door to the wall,
      continual bleeding,

and all the time that will which cancels enmity,
seeks its own Easter, arrives at the water-barrier;
must face it now, biting the lakeside ground;
      looks for its double,

the twin that must be met again, changeling need,
blazing in color somewhere, flying yellow
into the forest with its lucid edict:
      take to the world,

this is the honor of your flesh, the offering
of strangers, the faces of cities, honor of all your wish.
Immortal undoing! I say in my own voice.   These
    prophecies
      may all come true,

out of the beaten season.   I look in Rotten Lake
wait for the flame reflection, seeing only
the frec beast flickering black along my side
      animal of my need,

and cry I want! I want! rising among the world
to gain my converted wish, the amazing desire

that keeps me alive, though the face be still, be still,
and slow dilated heart know nothing but lack,
now I begin again the private rising,
the ride to survival of that consuming bird
beating, up from dead lakes, ascents of fire.

Third Elegy. The Fear of Form

Tyranny of method! the outrageous smile
seals the museums, pours a mob skidding
up to the formal staircase, stopped, mouths open.
And do they stare? They do.
At what? A sunset?

Blackness, obscurity, bravado were the three colors;
wit-play, movement, and wartime the three moments;
formal groups, fire, facility, the three hounds.

This was their art: a wall daubed like a face,
a penis or finger dipped in a red pigment.
The sentimental frown gave them their praise,
prized the wry color, the twisted definition,
and said, "You are right to copy."

But the car full of Communists put out hands and guns,
blew 1–2–3 on the horn before the
surrealist house, a spiral in Cataluña.

New combinations: set out materials now,
combine them again! the existence is the test.
What do you want? Lincoln blacking his lessons
in charcoal on an Indiana shovel?
or the dilettante, the impresario's beautiful skull
choosing the tulip crimson satin, the yellow satin
as the ballet dances its tenth time to the mirror?
Or the general's nephew, epaulets from birth,
run down the concourse, shouting Planes for Spain?

New methods, the staring circle given again
force, a phoenix of power, another Ancient
sits in his circle, while the plaster model
of an equation slowly rotates beneath him,
and all his golden compass leans.
Create an anti-sentimental: Sing!
"For children's art is not asylum art,
"there are these formal plays in living, for
"the equal triangle does not spell youth,
"the cube nor age, the sphere nor ever soul.
"Asylum art is never children's art.
"They cut the bones down, but the line remained.
"They cut the line for good, and reached the point
"blazing at the bottom of its night."

———

A man is walking, wearing the world, swearing
saying You damn fools come out into the open.
Whose dislocated wish? Whose terrors whine?
I'll fuse him straight.
The usable present starts my calendar.
Chorus of bootblacks, printers, collectors of shit.

Your witwork works, your artwork shatters, die.
Hammer up your abstractions. Divide, O zoo.
—He's a queer bird, a hero, a kangaroo.
What is he going to do?

He calls Rise out of cities, you memorable ghosts
scraps of an age whose choice is seen
to lie between evils.   Dazzle-paint the rest,
it burns my eyes with its acetylene.
Look through the wounds, mystic and human fly,
you spiritual unicorn, you clew of eyes.

Ghosts to approach the blood in fifteen cities.
Did you walk through the walls of the Comtesse de
        Noailles?
Was there a horror in Chicago?
Or ocean? Or ditches at the road. Or France,
while bearing guarding shadowing painting in Paris,
Picasso like an ass Picasso like a dragon Picasso like a
romantic movement
and immediately after, stations of swastikas
Prague and a thousand boys swing circles clean
girls by the thousand curve their arms together
geometries of wire
the barbed, starred
Heil

Will you have capitals with their tarnished countesses
their varnished cemetery life
vanished Picassos
or clean acceptable Copenhagen

or by God a pure high monument
white yellow and red
up against Minnesota?

Does the sea permit its dead to wear jewels?

Flame, fusion, defiance are your three guards,
the sphere, the circle, the cluster your three guides,
the bare, the blond and the bland are your three goads.

Adam, Godfinger, only these contacts function:
light and the high accompanied design,
contact of points   the fusion say of sex
the atombuster too along these laws.
Put in a sphere, here, at the focal joint,
he said, put it in. The moment is arrangement.
Currents washed through it, spun, blew white,
fused.   For! the sphere! proving!

This was the nightmare of a room alone,
the posture of grave figure, finger on other head,
he puts the finger of power on him,
optic of grandiose delusion.
All you adjacent and contagious points,
make room for fusion; fall,
you monuments, snow on your heads,
your power, your pockets, your dead parts.

Standing at midnight corners under corner-lamps
we wear the coat and the shadow of the coat.
The mind sailing over a scene lets light arrive

conspicuous sunrise, the knotted smoke rising,
the world with all its signatures visible.
Play of materials in balance,
carrying the strain of a new process.
Of the white root, the nature of the base,
contacts, making an index.
And do they stare? They do.
Our needs, our violences.
At what? Contortion of body and spirit.
To fuse it straight.

Fifth Elegy. A Turning Wind

Knowing the shape of the country.   Knowing the
    midway to
migrant fanatics, living that life, up with the dawn and
moving as long as the light lasts, and when the sun is
    falling
        to wait, still standing;

and when the black has come, at last lie down, too tired to
turn to each other, feeling only the land's demand under
    them.
Shape that exists not as permanent quality, but varies with
    even the movement of bone.

Even in skeletons, it depends on the choices of action.
A definite plan is visible.   We are either free-moving or
fixed to some ground.   The shape has no meaning
        outside of the function.

Fixed to Europe, the distant, adjacent, we lived, with the
        land—
promise of life of our own.   Course down the East—
        frontiers
meet you at every turn—the headlights find them, the
        plain's,
        and the solar cities'

recurrent centers.   And at the middle of the great
        world the wind
answers the shape of the country, a turning traveller
follows the hinge-line of coast, the first indefinite
        axis of symmetry

torn off from sympathy with the past and planted,
a primitive streak prefiguring the west, an ideal
which had to be modified for stability,
        to make it work.

Architecture is fixed not only by present needs but
also by ancestors.   The actual structure means a plan
        determined
by the nature of ancestors; its details are determined by
        function and interference.

There are these major divisions　:　for those attached
　　to the seafloor,
a fan at freedom, flexible, wavering, designed to catch
　　　food
from all directions.　For the sedentary, for those who
　　crouch and look,
　　　　radial symmetry,

spokes to all margins for support.　For those who want
　　movement,
this is achieved through bilateral symmetry only,
a spine and straight attack, all muscles working,
　　　　up and alive.

———

And there are years of roads, and centuries of need,
of walking along the shadow of a wall, of visiting houses,
hearing the birds trapped in the wall, the framework
　　trembling
　　　　with struggles of birds,

years of nightwalking in stranger cities, relost and
　　unnamed,
recurrent familiar rooms, furnished only with
　　nightmare,
recurrent loves, the glass eye of unreal ambition,
　　　　years of initiation,

of dishallucination on the diamond meadows,
seeing the distances of false capes ahead,
feeling the tide-following and turning wind,
　　　　travelling farther

under abrasive weather, to the bronzy river,
the rust, the brown, the terrible dead swamps,
the hanging moss the color of all the hanged,
      cities whose heels

ring out their news of hell upon all streets
churches where you betray yourself, pray ended desire,
white wooden houses of village squares.   Always one
    gesture:
      rejecting of backdrops.

These are the ritual years, whose lore is names of
    shapes,
Grabtown, Cockade Alley, Skid Row where jobless live,
their emblem a hitch-hiker with lips basted together,
    and marvel rivers,

the flooded James, a double rainbow standing over
    Richmond,
the remnant sky above the Cape Fear River, blue stain
    on red water,
the Waccamaw with its bone-trees, Piscataqua's rich
    mouth,
      red Sound and flesh of sand.

—A nation of refugees that will not learn its name;
still shows these mothers enduring, their hidden faces,
the cry of the hurt child at a high night-window,
      hand-to-hand warfare,

the young sitting in libraries at their only rest
or making love in the hallway under an orange bulb,
the boy playing baseball at Hungry Mother State Park,
       bestiaries of cities

and this shape, this meaning that promises seasonal joy.
Whose form is unquietness and yet the seeker of rest,
whose travelling hunger has range enough, its root
       grips through the world.

The austere fire-world of night : Gary or
      Bethlehem,
in sacred stacks of flame—or stainless morning,
anti-sunlight of lakes' reflection, matchlight on face,
      the thorny light of fireworks

lighting a way for the shape, this country of celebrations
deep in a passage of rebirth.   Adventures of countries,
adventures of travellers, visions, or Christ's adventures
      forever following him

lit by the night-light of history, persevering
into the incredible washed morning air.
The luisarne swamp is our guide and the glare ice,
      the glow of tracklights,

the lights winding themselves into a single beacon,
big whooping riders of night, a wind that whirls
all of our motives into a single stroke,
      shows us a country

of which the birds know mountains that we have not
      dreamed,
climbing these unsuspected slopes they fade.   Butte
      and pavilion
vanish into a larger scape, morning vaults all those hills
       rising on ranges

that stand gigantic on the roots of the world,
where points expand in pleasure of raw sweeping
gestures of joy, whose winds sweep down like stairs,
      and the felled forests

on hurricane ridges show a second growth.   The
      dances
of turkeys near storm, a pouring light, tornado
umbilical to earth, fountains of rain, a development
      controlled by centers,

until the organs of this anatomy are fleshed away at last
of gross, and determining self, develop a final structure
in isolation.   Masterpieces of happiness arrive,
      alive again in another land,

remembering pain, faces of suffering, but they know
      growth,
go through the world, hunger and rest desiring life.
Mountains are spines to their conquest, these wrecked
      houses
      (vines spiral the pillars)

are leaning their splintered sides on tornadoes, lifted
        careening
in wheels, in whirlwind, in a spool of power
drawing a spiral on the sun, drawing a sign of
        strength on the mountains,

the fusing stars lighting initiated cities.
The thin poor whiteness raining on the ground
forgotten in fickle eclipses, thunderbirds of dream
        following omens,

following charts of the moving constellations.
Charts of the country of all visions, imperishable
stars of our old dreams   :   process, which having
        neither
        sorrow nor joy

remains as promise, the embryo in the fire.
The tilted cities of America, fields of metal,
the seamless wheatfields, the current of cities running
        below our wings

promise that knowledge of systems which may bless.
May permit knowledge of self, a lover's wish of
        conversion
until the time when the dead lake rises in light,
the shape is organized in travelling space,
this hope of travel, to find the place again,
rest in the triumph of the reconceived,
lie down again together face to face.

Reading Time :   1 Minute 26 Seconds

The fear of poetry is the
fear   :   mystery and fury of a midnight street
of windows whose low voluptuous voice
issues, and after that there is no peace.

That round waiting moment in the
theatre   :   curtain rises, dies into the ceiling
and here is played the scene with the mother
bandaging a revealed son's head.   The bandage is torn off.
Curtain goes down.   And here is the moment of proof.

That climax when the brain acknowledges the world,
all values extended into the blood awake.
Moment of proof.   And as they say Brancusi did,
building his bird to extend through soaring air,
as Kafka planned stories that draw to eternity
through time extended.   And the climax strikes.

Love touches so, that months after the look of
blue stare of love, the footbeat on the heart
is translated into the pure cry of birds
following air-cries, or poems, the new scene.
Moment of proof.   That strikes long after act.

They fear it.   They turn away, hand up palm out
fending off moment of proof, the straight look, poem.
The prolonged wound-consciousness after the bullet's
        shot.
The prolonged love after the look is dead,
the yellow joy after the song of the sun.

Tree of Days

I was born in winter when
Europe heard the early guns,
when I was five, the drums
welcomed home the men.

The spring after my birth
a tree came out of the lake,
I laughed, for I could not speak;
the world was there to learn.

The richest season in
the headlines fell as I was ten,
but the crazies were forgotten,
the fine men, the bravest men.

When I had reached fifteen,
that pliant tree was dark,
breadlines haunted the parks—
the books tricked-in that scene.

No work in any town
when I was twenty, cured
the thin and desperate poor
from being forced alone.

Clear to half a brain
in a blind man's head,
war must follow that tide
of running milk and grain.

Now China's long begun,
that tree is dense and strong,
spreading, continuing—
and Austria; and Spain.

If some long unborn friend
looks at photos in pity,
we say, sure we were happy,
but it was not in the wind.

Half my twenties are gone
as the crazies take to the planes,
and fine men, the bravest men,
and the war goes on.

Paper Anniversary

The concert-hall was crowded the night of the Crash
but the wives were away; many mothers gone sick to
        their beds
or waiting at home for late extras and latest telephone
        calls
had sent their sons and daughters to hear music instead.

I came late with my father; and as the car flowed stop
I heard the Mozart developing through the door

where the latecomers listened; water-leap, season of
    coolness,
talisman of relief; but they worried, they did not hear.

Into the hall of formal rows and the straight-sitting seats
(they took out pencils, they muttered at the program's
    margins)
began the double concerto, Brahms' season of fruit
but they could not meet it with love; they were lost with
    their fortunes.

In that hall was no love where love was often felt
reaching for music, or for the listener beside:
orchids and violins—precision dances of pencils
rode down the paper as the music rode.

Intermission with its spill of lights found heavy
breathing and failure pushing up the aisles,
or the daughters of failure greeting each other under
the eyes of an old man who has gone mad and fails.

And this to end the cars, the trips abroad, the summer
countries of palmtrees, toy moneys, curt affairs,
ending all music for the evening-dress audience.
Fainting in telephone booth, the broker swears.

"I was cleaned out at Forty—" "No golf tomorrow"
    "Father!"
but fathers there were none, only a rout of men
stampeded in a flaming circle; and they return
from the telephones and run down the velvet lane

as the lights go down and the Stravinsky explodes
spasms of rockets to levels near delight,
and the lawyer thinks of his ostrich-feather wife
lying alone, and knows it is getting late.

He journeys up the aisle, and as Debussy begins,
drowning the concert-hall, many swim up and out,
distortions of water carry their bodies through
the deformed image of a crippled heart.

The age of the sleepless and the sealed arrives.
The music spent.   Hard-breathing, they descend,
wait at the door or at the telephone.
While from the river streams a flaw of wind,

washing our sight; while all the fathers lie
heavy upon their graves, the line of cars progresses
toward the blue park, and the lobby darkens, and we
go home again to the insane governess.

The night is joy, and the music was joy alive,
alive is joy, but it will never be
upon this scene upon these fathers these cars
for the windows already hold photography

of the drowned faces the fat the unemployed—
pressed faces lie upon the million glass
and the sons and daughters turn their startled faces
and see that startled face.

From the Duck-Pond to the Carousel

Playing a phonograph record of a windy morning
you gay   you imitation summer
                let's see you slice up the Park
in green from the lake drawn bright in silver salt
while the little girl playing   (in iodine and pink)
tosses her crumbs and they all rise to catch
lifting up their white and saying Quack.

O you pastoral lighting what are you getting away with?
Wound-up lovers   fidgeting balloons   and a popsicle
        man
running up the road on the first day of spring.
And the baby carriages whose nurses with flat heels
(for sufferance is the badge of all their tribe)
mark turning sunlight on far avenues
etch beacons on the grass.   You strenuous baby
rushing up to the wooden horses
with their stiff necks, their eyes,
and all their music!

Fountains!   sheepfolds!   merry-go-round!
The seal that barking slips Pacifics dark-
diving into his well until up! with a fish!
The tiglon resembling his Siberian sire,
ice-cream and terraces and twelve o'clock.
O mister with the attractive moustache,
        How does it happen to be you?
Mademoiselle in   cinnamon   zoo,
            Hello,   hello.

Judith

This is a dark woman at a telephone
thinking 'brown blood, brown blood' and calling
numbers, saying to her friend, "I will be gone
"a month or two," breaking a weekend saying
"I will be back in a week," in an undertone
to her doctor, "I will take care of the child,
"I may be back within the year," thinking alone
'brown blood' and staring hard at the furniture
remembering the nightmares of a room
she leaves, forever clamped at her breastbone.

This is a woman recalling waters of Babylon,
seeing all charted life as a homicide map
flooded up to the X which marks her life's
threatened last waterline.   Safety now for her husband,
no taint—brown blood for him, the naked blond,
the tall and safe.   For her, the bottomless ship
inviting to voyage—the sly advertisement,
as the enemy in war invites to luxury:
"Our side has its meat, wine, and cigarettes."
Prediction of no safety for the bone.

This is a woman putting away close pain,
child of a stolid mother whose family runs wild,
abandons fear, abandons legend; while the insane
French peasant is caught, stalking and barking Heil,
fire, anemia, famine, the long smoky madness
a broken century cannot reconcile.
Agons of blood, brown blood, and a dark woman

leaves the blond country with a backward look,
adventures into the royal furious dark
already spread from Kishinev to York.

At the green sources of the Amazon
a bird develops, who repeats his race
whole in a lifetime; hatched with primitive claws
he grows and can absorb them and is grown
to a green prime of feathers.   This is known.
A woman sitting at a telephone
repeats her race, hopes for the trap's defence.
Defenders rumored nothing but skeleton.
Applause of news.   Suicides reaching for
ritual certainty in their last impatience.

These dragon-surrounded young cannot obtain,
and the white children who become unreal,
live responsive as smoke and travel alone,
wish revocation of fugitives and banned,
know sun-roar, fatal telephones, the hand
palm placing out, the face wanting its rant.
Cry to the newborn, the youngest in the world
for a new twisting wind to be all winds
to cancel this, rejuvenating rain
to wash it away, forces to fight it down.

A dark-faced woman at a telephone
answered by silence and cruelest dragon-silence;
she knows the weakness of the dim and alone,
compunctive bitter essence of the wound,
the world-spike that is driven through all our hearts.

She will go like a woman sweated from a stone
out from these boundaries, while a running cloud
in that bruised night no bigger than a brain
joins in a cloud-race over the flat of sky
in persecution of the whitened moon.

GIBBS

It was much later in his life he rose
in the professors' room, the frail bones rising
among that fume of mathematical meaning,
symbols, the language of symbols, literature . . . threw
air, simple life, in the dead lungs of their meeting,
said, "Mathematics *is* a language."

Withdrew.   Into a silent world beyond New Haven,
the street-fights gone, the long youth of undergraduate
riots down Church Street, initiation violence,
secret societies gone   :   a broken-glass isolation,
bottles smashed flat, windows out, street-fronts
    broken   :

                to quiet,
the little portico, wrought-iron and shutters' house.
A usable town, a usable tradition.
                    In war or politics.

Not science.
              Withdrew.
                            Civil War generates, but
Not here. Tutors Latin after his doctorate
when all of Yale is disappearing south.
There is no disorganization, for there is no passion.
Condense, he is thinking.   Concentrate, restrict.
This is the state permits the whole to stand,
the whole which is simpler than any of its parts.
And the mortars fired, the tent-lines, lines of trains,
earthworks, breastworks of war, field-hospitals,
Whitman forever saying, "Identify."
Gibbs saying
              "I wish to know systems."

To be in this work.   Prepare an apocryphal
cool life in which nothing is not discovery
and all is given, levelly, after clearest
most disciplined research.
                            The German years
of voyage, calmer than Kant in Koenigsberg, to states
where laws are passed and truth's a daylight gift.

Return to a house inheriting Julia's keys,
sister receiving all the gifts of the world,
white papers on your desk.
                            Spiritual gift
she never took.
              Books of discovery,
haunted by steam, ghost of the disembodied engine,
industrialists in their imperious designs

made flower an age to be driven far by this
serene impartial acumen.
                            Years of driving
his sister's coach in the city, knowing the
rose of direction loosing its petals down
atoms and galaxies.   Diffusion's absolute.
Phases of matter! The shouldering horses pass
turnings (snow, water, steam) echoing plotted curves,
statues of diagrams, the forms of schemes
to stand white on a table, real as phase,
or as the mountainous summer curves when he
under New Hampshire lay while shouldering night
came down upon him then with all its stars.
Gearing that power-spire to the wide air.
Exacting symbols of rediscovered worlds.

Through evening New Haven drove.   The yellow
    window
of Sloane Lab all night shone.

Shining an image whole, as a streak of brightness
bland on the quartz, light-blade on Iceland spar
doubled! and the refraction carrying fresh clews.
Withdrew.
            It will be an age of experiment,
or mysticism, anyway vastest assumption.
He makes no experiments. Impregnable retires.
Anyone having these desires will make these researches.
Laws are the gifts of their systems, and the man
in constant tension of experience drives

moments of coexistence into light.
It is the constitution of matter I must touch.

Deduction from deduction   :   entropy,
heat flowing down a gradient of nature,
perpetual glacier driving down the side
of the known world in an equilibrium tending
to uniformity, the single dream.
                         He binds
himself to know the public life of systems.
Look through the wounds of law
at the composite face of the world.

               If Scott had known,
he would not die at the Pole, he would have been
saved, and again saved—here, gifts from overseas,
and grapes in January past Faustus' grasp.
Austerity, continence, veracity, the full truth flowing
not out from the beginning and the base,
but from accords of components whose end is truth.
Thought resting on these laws enough becomes
an image of the world, restraint among
breaks manacles, breaks the known life before
Gibbs' pale and steady eyes.
                      He knew the composite
many-dimensioned spirit, the phases of its face,
found the tremendous level of the world,
Energy   :   Constant, but entropy, the spending,
tends toward a maximum—a "mixed-up-ness,"
and in this end of levels to which we drive

in isolation, to which all systems tend,
Withdraw, he said clearly.

The soul says to the self　:　I will withdraw,
the self saying to the soul　:　I will withdraw,
and soon they are asleep together
spiralling through one dream.

　　　　　　　　　　　　Withdrew, but in
his eager imperfect timidities, rose and dared
sever waterspouts, bring the great changing world
time makes more random, into its unity.

ANN BURLAK

Let her be seen, a voice on a platform, heard
as a city is heard in its prophetic sleep when
one shadow hangs over one side of a total wall
of houses, factories, stacks, and on the faces
around her tallies, shadow from one form.

An open square shields the voice, reflecting it
to faces who receive its reflections of light as
change on their features. She stands alone, sending
her voice out to the edges, seeing approach people
to make the ring ragged, to fill in blacker
answers.
　　　　　This is an open square of the lit world
whose dark sky over hills rimmed white with evening
squares lofts where sunset lies in dirty patterns
and rivers of mill-towns beating their broken bridges

as under another country full of air.
Dark offices evening reaches where letters take the light
even from palest faces over script.
Many abandon machines, shut off the looms,
hurry on glooming cobbles to the square. And many
are absent, as in the sky about her face, the birds
retreat from charcoal rivers and fly far.

The words cluster about the superstition mountains.
The sky breaks back over the torn and timid
her early city whose stacks along the river
flourished darkness over all, whose mottled sky
shielded the faces of those asleep in doorways
spread dark on narrow fields through which the father
comes home without meat, the forest in the ground
whose trees are coal, the lurching roads of autumn
where the flesh of the eager hangs, heavier by
its thirty bullets, barbed on wire.   Truckdrivers
swing ungrazed trailers past, the woman in the fog
can never speak her poems of unemployment,
the brakeman slows the last freight round the curve.
And riveters in their hardshell fling short fiery
steel, and the servant groans in his narrow room,
and the girl limps away from the door of the shady
        doctor.
Or the child new-born into a company town
whose life can be seen at birth as child, woman, widow.
The neighbor called in to nurse the baby of a spy,
the schoolboy washing off the painted word
"scab" on the front stoop, his mother watering flowers
pouring the milk-bottle of water from the ledge,

who stops in horror, seeing.   The grandmother going
down to her cellar with a full clothes-basket,
turns at the shot, sees men running past brick,
smoke-spurt and fallen face.
                              She speaks of these:
the chase down through the canal, the filling-station,
stones through the windshield. The woman in the bank
who topples, the premature birth brought on by
     tear-gas,
the charge leaving its gun slow-motion, finding those
who sit at windows knowing what they see;
who look up at the door, the brutalized face appraising
strangers with holsters; little blackened boys
with their animal grins, quick hands salvaging coal
among the slag of patriotic hills.

She knows the field of faces at her feet,
remembrances of childhood, likenesses of parents,
a system of looms in constellation whirled,
disasters dancing.
                    And behind her head
the world of the unpossessed, steel mills in snow
     flaming,
nine o'clock towns whose deputies' overnight power
hurls waste into killed eyes, whose guns predict
mirages of order, an empty coat before the blind.
Doorways within which nobody is at home.
The spies who wait for the spy at the deserted crossing,
a little dead since they are going to kill.
Those women who stitch their lives to their machines
and daughters at the symmetry of looms.

She speaks to the ten greatest American women:
The anonymous farmer's wife, the anonymous clubbed
        picket,
the anonymous Negro woman who held off the guns,
the anonymous prisoner, anonymous cotton-picker
trailing her robe of sack in a proud train,
anonymous writer of these and mill-hand, anonymous
        city walker,
anonymous organizer, anonymous binder of the illegally
        wounded,
anonymous feeder and speaker to anonymous squares.

She knows their faces, their impatient songs
of passionate grief risen, the desperate music
poverty makes, she knows women cut down
by poverty, by stupid obscure days,
their moments over the dishes, speaks them now,
wrecks with the whole necessity of the past
behind the debris, behind the ordinary
smell of coffee, the ravelling clean wash,
the turning to bed, undone among savage night
planning and unplanning seasons of happiness
broken in dreams or in the jaundiced morning
over a tub or over a loom or over
the tired face of death.
                    She knows
the songs   :   *Hope to die, Mo I try, I comes out,*
Owin boss mo, I comes out, Lawd, Owin boss mo
food, money and life.
                    Praise breakers,
praise the unpraised who cannot speak their name.

Their asking what they need as unbelieved
as a statue talking to a skeleton.
They are the animals who devour their mother
from need, and they know in their bodies other places,
their minds are cities whose avenues are named
each after a foreign city.　　They fall when cities fall.

They have the cruelty and sympathy of those
whose texture is the stress of existence woven
into revenge, the crime we all must claim.
They hold the old world in their new world's arms.
And they are the victims, all the splinters of war
run through their eyes, their black escaping face
and runaway eyes are the Negro in the subway
whose shadowy detective brings his stick
down on the naked head as the express pulls in,
swinging in locomotive roars on skull.
They are the question to the ambassador
long-jawed and grim, they stand on marble, waiting
to ask how the terms of the strike have affected him.
Answer: "I've never seen snow before. It's marvellous."
They stand with Ann Burlak in the rotunda, knowing
her insistent promise of life, remembering
the letter of the tear-gas salesman　:　"I hope
"this strike develops and a damn bad one too.
"We need the money."

　　　　　　　　　This is the boundary
behind a speaker　:　Main Street and railroad tracks,
post office, furniture store.　　The soft moment before
　　　storm.
Since there are many years.

And the first years were the years of need,
the bleeding, the dragged foot, the wilderness,
and the second years were the years of bread
fat cow, square house, favorite work,
and the third years are the years of death.
The glittering eye all golden. Full of tears.
Years when the enemy is in our street,
and liberty, safe in the people's hands,
is never safe and peace is never safe.

Insults of attack arrive, insults
of mutilation.   She knows the prophetic past,
many have marched behind her, and she knows
Rosa whose face drifts in the black canal,
the superstitions of a tragic winter
when children, their heads together, put on tears.
The tears fall at their throats, their chains are made
of tears, and as bullets melted and as bombs let down
upon the ominous cities where she stands
fluid and conscious.   Suddenly perceives
the world will never daily prove her words,
but her words live, they issue from this life.
She scatters clews.   She speaks from all these faces
and from the center of a system of lives
who speak the desire of worlds moving unmade
saying, "Who owns the world?" and waiting for the cry.

Ajanta

I. The Journey

Came in my full youth to the midnight cave
Nerves ringing; and this thing I did alone.
Wanting my fulness and not a field of war,
For the world considered annihilation, a star
Called Wormwood rose and flickered, shattering
Bent light over the dead boiling up in the ground,
The biting yellow of their corrupted lives
Streaming to war, denying all our words.
Nothing was left among the tainted weather
But world-walking and shadowless Ajanta.
Hallucination and the metal laugh
In clouds, and the mountain-spectre riding storm.
Nothing was certain but a moment of peace,
A hollow behind the unbreakable waterfall.
All the way to the cave, the teeming forms of death,
And death, the price of the body, cheap as air.
I blessed my heart on the expiation journey
For it had never been unable to suffer:
When I met the man whose face looked like the future,
When I met the whore with the dying red hair,
The child myself who is my murderer.
So came I between heaven and my grave

Past the serene smile of the *voyeur*, to
This cave where the myth enters the heart again.

II. The Cave

Space to the mind, the painted cave of dream.
This is not a womb, nothing but good emerges:
This is a stage, neither unreal nor real,
Where the walls are the world, the rocks and palaces
Stand on a borderland of blossoming ground.
If you stretch your hand, you touch the slope of the
        world
Reaching in interlaced gods, animals, and men.
There is no background.   The figures hold their peace
In a web of movement.   There is no frustration,
Every gesture is taken, everything yields connections.
The heavy sensual shoulders, the thighs, the blood-born
        flesh
And earth turning into color, rocks into their crystals,
Water to sound, fire to form; life flickers
Uncounted into the supple arms of love.
The space of these walls is the body's living space;
Tear open your ribs and breathe the color of time
Where nothing leads away, the world comes forward
In flaming sequences.   Pillars and prisms.   Riders
And horses and the figures of consciousness,
Red cow grows long, goes running through the world.
Flung into movement in carnal purity,
These bodies are sealed—warm lip and crystal hand
In a jungle of light.   Color-sheeted, seductive
Foreboding eyelid lowered on the long eye,

Fluid and vulnerable.   The spaces of the body
Are suddenly limitless, and riding flesh
Shapes constellations over the golden breast,
Confusion of scents and illuminated touch—
Monster touch, the throat printed with brightness,
Wide outlined gesture where the bodies ride.
Bells, and the spirit flashing.   The religious bells,
Bronze under the sunlight like breasts ringing,
Bronze in the closed air, the memory of walls,
Great sensual shoulders in the web of time.

III. *Les Tendresses Bestiales*

A procession of caresses alters the ancient sky
Until new constellations are the body shining:
There's the Hand to steer by, there the horizon Breast,
And the Great Stars kindling the fluid hill.
All the rooms open into magical boxes,
Nothing is tilted, everything flickers
Sexual and exquisite.
The panther with its throat along my arm
Turns black and flows away.
Deep in all streets passes a faceless whore
And the checkered men are whispering one word.
The face I know becomes the night-black rose.
The sharp face is now an electric fan
And says one word to me.
The dice and the alcohol and the destruction
Have drunk themselves and cast.
Broken bottle of loss, and the glass
Turned bloody into the face.

Now the scene comes forward, very clear.
Dream-singing, airborne, surrenders the recalled,
The gesture arrives riding over the breast,
Singing, singing, tender atrocity,
The silver derelict wearing fur and claws.
O love, I stood under the apple branch,
I saw the whipped bay and the small dark islands,
And night sailing the river and the foghorn's word.
My life said to you: I want to love you well.
The wheel goes back and I shall live again,
But the wave turns, my birth arrives and spills
Over my breast the world bearing my grave,
And your eyes open in earth.   You touched my life.
My life reaches the skin, moves under your smile,
And your throat and your shoulders and your face and
     your thighs
Flash.
                    I am haunted by interrupted acts,
Introspective as a leper, enchanted
By a repulsive clew,
A gross and fugitive movement of the limbs.
Is this the love that shook the lights to flame?
Sheeted avenues thrash in the wind,
Torn streets, the savage parks.
I am plunged deep.   Must find the midnight cave.

IV. Black Blood

A habit leading to murder, smoky laughter
Hated at first, but necessary later.
Alteration of motives.   To stamp in terror
Around the deserted harbor, down the hill
Until the woman laced into a harp
Screams and screams and the great clock strikes,
Swinging its giant figures past the face.
The Floating Man rides on the ragged sunset
Asking and asking.   Do not say, Which loved?
Which was beloved? Only, Who most enjoyed?
Armored ghost of rage, screaming and powerless.
Only find me and touch my blood again.
Find me.   A girl runs down the street
Singing Take me, yelling Take me Take
Hang me from the clapper of a bell
And you as hangman ring it sweet tonight,
For nothing clean in me is more than cloud
Unless you call it.   —As I ran I heard
A black voice beating among all that blood:
"Try to live as if there were a God."

V. The Broken World

Came to Ajanta cave, the painted space of the breast,
The real world where everything is complete,
There are no shadows, the forms of incompleteness.
The great cloak blows in the light, rider and horse
    arrive,
The shoulders turn and every gift is made.

No shadows fall.   There is no source of distortion.
In our world, a tree casts the shadow of a woman,
A man the shadow of a phallus, a hand raised
The shadow of the whip.
Here everything is itself,
Here all may stand
On summer earth.
Brightness has overtaken every light,
And every myth netted itself in flesh.
New origins, and peace given entire
And the spirit alive.
In the shadowless cave
The naked arm is raised.

Animals arrive,
Interlaced, and gods
Interlaced, and men
Flame-woven.
I stand and am complete.
Crawls from the door,
Black at my two feet
The shadow of the world.

World, not yet one,
Enters the heart again.
The naked world, and the old noise of tears,
The fear, the expiation and the love,
A world of the shadowed and alone.

The journey, and the struggles of the moon.

Child in the Great Wood

It is all much worse than I dreamed.
The trees are all here,
Trunk, limb, and leaf,
Nothing beyond belief
In danger's atmosphere
And the underbrush is cursed.
But the animals,
Some are as I have dreamed,
Appear and do their worst
Until more animals
With recognizable faces
Arrive and take their places
And do their worst.

It is all a little like dreaming,
But this forest is silent,
This acts out anxiety
In a midnight stillness.
My blood that sparkles in me
Cannot endure this voiceless
Forest, this is not sleep
Not peace but a lack of words.
And the mechanical birds
Wing, claw, and sharpened eye.
I cannot see their sky.

Even this war is not unlike the dream,
But in the dream-war there were armies,
Armies and armor and death's etiquette,

Here there are no troops and no protection,
Only this wrestling of the heart
And a demon-song that goes
For sensual friction
Is largely fiction
And partly fact
And so is tact
And so is love,
And so is love.

The thin leaves chatter. There is a sound at last
Begun at last by the demon-song.
Behind the wildest trees I see the men together
Confessing their lives and the women together.
But really I cannot hear the words.   I cannot hear the
    song.
This may still be my dream
But the night seems very long.

Darkness Music

The days grow and the stars cross over
    And my wild bed turns slowly among the stars.

Drunken Girl

Do you know the name of the average animal?
Not the dog,
    Nor the green-beaded frog,

Nor the white ocean monster lying flat—
    Lower than that.
The curling one who comes out in the storm—
The middle one's the worm.

Lift up your face, my love, lift up your mouth,
Kiss me and come to bed
    And do not bow your head
Longer on what is bad or what is good—
    The dead are terribly misunderstood,
And sin and godhead are in the worm's blind eye,
We'll come to averages by and by.

The Minotaur

Trapped, blinded, led; and in the end betrayed
Daily by new betrayals as he stays
Deep in his labyrinth, shaking and going mad.
Betrayed.   Betrayed.   Raving, the beaten head
Heavy with madness, he stands, half-dead and proud.
No one again will ever see his pride.
No one will find him by walking to him straight
But must be led circuitously about,
Calling to him and close and, losing the subtle thread,
Lose him again; while he waits, brutalized
By loneliness.   Later, afraid
Of his own suffering.   At last, savage and made
Ravenous, ready to prey upon the race
If it so much as learn the clews of blood
Into his pride his fear his glistening heart.

Now is the patient deserted in his fright
And love carrying salvage round the world
Lost in a crooked city; roundabout,
By the sea, the precipice, all the fantastic ways
Betrayal weaves its trap; loneliness knows the thread,
And the heart is lost, lost, trapped, blinded and led,
Deserted at the middle of the maze.

Gift-Poem

The year in its cold beginning
Promises more than cold;
The old contrary rhyming
Will never again hold—
The great moon in its timing
Making the empty sky
A continent of light
Creates fine bombing weather,
Assures a safer flight
For fliers, and many will die
Who in their backwardness
Cannot leave the ground.
Weather is not what it was:
The losers are not winning,
The lost will never be found.
The year in its cold beginning
Finds us a good deal farther
From our good weather
Than we had ever dreamed.

Darling, dead words sublimed
May be read out loud at last:
The legendary past
Cannot scare us again.
This is what I have known
After a New Year's Eve
Of a desperate time.
There will be great sorrow,
Great pain, and detailed joy,
The gladness of flowering
Minutes, green living leaf.
You recommend me grief:
There will be no more grief;
Terrible battle that tears the world apart,
Terrible health that takes the world to bed,
Sickness that, broken, jets across the room
Into the future time;
Not the mild ways of grief,
Mourning that feels at home.

I see your gardens from here,
I see on your terraces
The shadowy awful regiment;
The weak man, the impossible man,
The curly-headed impotent
Whose failure did not reach his face,
And then the struggle for grace, and then
The school'd attenuated men.

I know you are moved by these:
The vice of self-desire

That does not lead to crime,
Leads to no action, is rather
Liquid seductive fire
Before the final blame
When there is no forgiveness.

And many lovers fail to love,
Lose the ability to move
Before the supernatural fear
Calls to the natural need
Come to the feast and feed
On a supernatural meal:
The taproot and the sacrifice.
Nothing can arrive to heal
The dead wish, the living face
That sees its disgrace and loss,
But the loss of its dear wish:
The word spoken across
Distance and loneliness—
Communication to the flesh.

There will be small joy:
There will be great rage,
Do not tell me the feeble
Grief of the very weak;
Only turn, only speak.
I see all the possible ends.
But the impossible;
I know it in its weakness,
Unborn and unprized,
It still commands my faith.

And then I remember the page
Of other words for death.
Then I remember the voices,
The voice not recognized
Or overheard too soon;
Rejected offerings,
Letter and telephone,
And I think of the bombing weather
Fine in the full of the moon.

I think of the big moon
Plain on the gardens,
And the clews of the year.
The haunted gardens wear it,
Knowledge like furniture;
The white frame of the spirit
Whose painting is naked fear.

The girl whose father raped her first
Should have used a little knife;
Failing that, her touch is cursed
By the omissive sin for life;
This bitter year's event and change
Turned to personal revenge.
Paint out the tortured painting,
The scene is too well done
But this processional
Must find some other saint,
Must find some other colors,
Some better expiation
Even more strange.

Murder is not the link;
Meaning must set it right.
Never recommend me grief
Nor deny my horror's straightness,
Early and late I see
The fire in the leaf
The minute's appetite.
If horror fire and change
Bring us our success
The word is indeed lost—
If the frosty world
Start its newest year
In fear and loss and belief,
Something may yet be safe.

Joy may touch the eyes again,
Night restore the walls of sleep,
Ease the will's incessant strain
And the forehead and the breast
And the lung where death lies sleeping.
Darling, if there should be tears,
They'll be no easy movie weeping,
Never the soft tears of grief
That go as simply as they start;
The rage and horror of the heart
In conflict with its love.

January 1941

Leg in a Plaster Cast

When at last he was well enough to take the sun
He leaned on the nearest railing and summed up his
     sins,
Criminal weaknesses, deeds done and undone.
He felt he was healing.   He guessed he was sane.

The convalescent gleam upon his skin,
With his supported leg and an unknown
Recovery approaching let him black out pain.
The world promised recovery from his veins.

People said "Sin"; in the park everyone
Mentioned one miracle: "We must all be reborn."
Across an accidental past the horns
Blasted through stone and barriers of sense

And the sound of a plaster cast knocking on stone.
He recognized the sound of fearful airmen
Returning, forerunners, and he could not run.
He saw they were not flying home alone.

He stood in a down-torn town of men and women
Whose wasted days poured on their heads as rain,
As sin, as fire—too lame, too late to turn,
For there, the air, everywhere full of planes.

Bubble of Air

The bubbles in the blood sprang free,
crying from roots, from Darwin's beard.
The angel of the century
stood on the night and would be heard;
turned to my dream of tears and sang:
Woman, American, and Jew,
three guardians watch over you,
three lions of heritage
resist the evil of your age:
life, freedom, and memory.
And all the dreams cried from the camps
and all the steel of torture rang.
The angel of the century
stood on the night and cried the great
notes Give Create and Fight—
while war
runs through your veins, while life
a bubble of air stands in your throat,
answer the silence of the weak:
Speak!

I

Women and poets see the truth arrive.
Then it is acted out,
The lives are lost, and all the newsboys shout.

Horror of cities follows, and the maze
Of compromise and grief.
The feeble cry Defeat be my belief.

All the strong agonized men
Wear the hard clothes of war,
Try to remember what they are fighting for.

But in dark weeping helpless moments of peace
Women and poets believe and resist forever:
The blind inventor finds the underground river.

IV. Sestina

Coming to Spain on the first day of the fighting,
Flame in the mountains, and the exotic soldiers,
I gave up ideas of strangeness, but now, keeping
All I profoundly hoped for, I saw fearing
Travellers and the unprepared and the fast-changing
Foothills.   The train stopped in a silver country.

Coast-water lit the valleys of this country—
All mysteries stood human in the fighting.
We came from far.   We wondered, Were they
      changing,
Our mild companions, turning into soldiers?
But the cowards were persistent in their fearing,
Each of us narrowed to one wish he was keeping.

There was no change of heart here; we were keeping
Our deepest wish, meeting with hope this country.
The enemies among us went on fearing
The frontier was too far behind.   The fighting
Was clear to us all at last.   The belted soldiers
Vanished into white hills that dark was changing.

The train stood naked in flowery midnight changing
All complex marvellous hope to war, and keeping
Among us only the main wish, and the soldiers.
We loved each other, believed in the war; this country
Meant to us the arrival of the fighting
At home; we began to know what we were fearing.

As continents broke apart, we saw our fearing
Reflect our nations' fears; we acted as changing
Cities at home would act, with one wish, fighting
This threat or falling under it; we were keeping
The knowledge of fiery promises; this country
Struck at our lives, struck deeper than its soldiers.

Those who among us were sure became our soldiers.
The dreams of peace resolved our subtle fearing.

This was the first day of war in a strange country.
Free Catalonia offered that day our changing
Age's hope and resistance, held in its keeping
The war this age must win in love and fighting.

This first day of fighting showed us all men as soldiers.
It offered one wish for keeping.   Hope.   Deep fearing.
Our changing spirits awake in the soul's country.

VII

To be a Jew in the twentieth century
Is to be offered a gift.   If you refuse,
Wishing to be invisible, you choose
Death of the spirit, the stone insanity.
Accepting, take full life.   Full agonies:
Your evening deep in labyrinthine blood
Of those who resist, fail, and resist; and God
Reduced to a hostage among hostages.

The gift is torment.   Not alone the still
Torture, isolation; or torture of the flesh.
That may come also.   But the accepting wish,
The whole and fertile spirit as guarantee
For every human freedom, suffering to be free,
Daring to live for the impossible.

IX

Among all the waste there are the intense stories
And tellers of stories.   One saw a peasant die.

One guarded a soldier through disease.   And one
Saw all the women look at each other in hope.
And came back, saying, "All things must be known."

They come home to the rat-faced investigator
Who sneers and asks, "Who is your favorite poet?"
Voices of scissors and grinders asking their questions:
"How did you ever happen to be against fascism?"
And they remember the general's white hair,
The food-administrator, alone and full of tears.

They come home to the powder-plant at twilight,
The girls emerging like discolored shadows.
But this is a land where there is time, and time;
This is the country where there is time for thinking.
"Is he a 'fellow-traveler'?—   No.   —Are you
        sure?   —No."
The fear.   Voices of clawhammers and spikes clinking.

If they bomb the cities, they must offer the choice.
Taking away the sons, they must create a reason.
The cities and women cry in a frightful voice,
"I care not who makes the laws, let me make the sons."
But look at their eyes, like drinking animals'
Full of assurance and flowing with reward.
The seeds of answering are in their voice.
The spirit lives, against the time's disease.
You little children, come down out of your mothers
And tell us about peace.

I hear the singing of the lives of women,
The clear mystery, the offering and pride.
But here also the orange lights of a bar, and an
Old biddy singing inside:

Rain and tomorrow more
They say there will be rain
They lean together and tell
The sorrow of the loin.

Telling each other, saying
"But can you understand?"
They recount separate sorrows.
Throat.   Forehead.   Hand.

On the bars and walls of buildings
They passed when they were young
They vomit out their pain,
The sorrow of the lung.

Who would suspect it of women?
They have not any rest.
Sad dreams of the belly, of the lip,
Of the deep warm breast.

All sorrows have their place in flesh,
All flesh will with its sorrow die—
All but the patch of sunlight over,
Over the sorrowful sunlit eye.

Eyes of Night-Time

On the roads at night I saw the glitter of eyes:
my dark around me let shine one ray;   that black
allowed their eyes   :   spangles in the cat's, air in the
    moth's eye shine,
mosaic of the fly, ruby-eyed beetle, the eyes that never
    weep,
the horned toad sitting and its tear of blood,
fighters and prisoners in the forest, people
aware in this almost total dark, with the difference,
the one broad fact of light.

Eyes on the road at night, sides of a road like rhyme;
the floor of the illumined shadow sea
and shallows with their assembling flash and show
of sight, root, holdfast, eyes of the brittle stars.
And your eyes in the shadowy red room,
scent of the forest entering, various time
calling and the light of wood along the ceiling
and over us birds calling and their circuit eyes.
And in our bodies the eyes of the dead and the living
giving us gifts at hand, the glitter of all their eyes.

Salamander

Red leaf.   And beside it, a red leaf alive
flickers, the eyes set wide in the leaf head,
small broad chest, a little taper of flame for tail
moving a little among the leaves like fear.

Flickering red in the wet week of rain
while a bird falls safely through his mile of air.

Green Limits

My limits crowd around me
like years, like those I loved
whose narrow hope could never
carry themselves.

My limits stand beside me
like those two widowed aunts
who from an empty beach
tore me into the wave.

Green over my low head
the surf threw itself down
tall as my aunts whose hands
locked me past help.

The sand was far behind
and rushing underfoot

water and fear and childhood,
surf of love.

Green limits walled me, water
stood higher than I saw—
glass walls, fall back!   let me
dive and be saved.

My limits stand inside me
forever like that wave
on which I ride at last
over and under me.

Foghorn in Horror

I know that behind these walls is the city, over these
    rooftops is the sun.
But I see black clothes only and white clothes with the
    fog running in
and all their shadows.
Every minute the sound of the harbor
intruding on horror with a bellow of horror:
blu-a!   blu-aa!   Ao. . . .

I try to write to you, but here too I meet failure.
It has a face like mine.
Silence and in me and over the water
only the bellowing,
Niobe howling for her life and her children.

Did you think this sorrow of women was a graceful
    thing?
Horrible Niobe down on her knees:
Blu-a!   Blu-aa!   Ao. . . .

Thirty years, and my full strength, and all I touch has
    failed.
I sit and see
the black clothes on the line are beautiful, the sky
    drifting away.
The white clothes of the fog beyond me, beautiful, and
    the shadows.
Blu-aa!   Blu-aa!   AO.

Then I Saw What the Calling Was

All the voices of the wood called "Muriel!"
but it was soon solved;   it was nothing, it was not for me.
The words were a little like Mortal and More and
    Endure
and a word like Real, a sound like Health or Hell.
Then I saw what the calling was   :   it was the road I
    traveled, the clear
time and these colors of orchards, gold behind gold and
    the full
shadow behind each tree and behind each slope.   Not
    to me
the calling, but to anyone, and at last I saw   :   where

the road lay through sunlight and many voices and the
    marvel
orchards, not for me, not for me, not for me.
I came into my clear being;   uncalled, alive, and sure.
Nothing was speaking to me, but I offered and all was
    well.

And then I arrived at the powerful green hill.

Nine Poems
for the unborn child

II

They came to me and said, "There is a child."
Fountains of images broke through my land.
My swords, my fountains spouted past my eyes
And in my flesh at last I saw.   Returned
To when we drove in the high forest, and earth
Turned to glass in the sunset where the wild
Trees struck their roots as deep and visible
As their high branches, the double planted world.

"There is no father," they came and said to me.
—I have known fatherless children, the searching, walk
The world, look at all faces for their father's life.
Their choice is death or the world.   And they do
    choose.
Earn their brave set of bone, the seeking marvelous look
Of those who lose and use and know their lives.

VII

You will enter the world where death by fear and
    explosion
Is waited;   longed for by many;   by all dreamed.
You will enter the world where various poverty
Makes thin the imagination and the bone.
You will enter the world where birth is walled about,
Where years are walled journeys, death a walled-in act.
You will enter the world which eats itself
Naming faith, reason, naming love, truth, fact.

You in your dark lake moving darkly now
Will leave a house that time makes, times to come
Enter the present, where all the deaths and all
The old betrayals have come home again.
World where again Judas, the little child,
May grow and choose.   You will enter the world.

F.O.M.

the death of Matthiessen

It was much stronger than they said. Noisier.
Everything in it more colored. Wilder.
More at the center calm.
Everything was more violent than ever they said,
Who tried to guard us from suicide and life.
We in our wars were more than they had told us.
Now that descent figures stand about the horizon,
I have begun to see the living faces,
The storm, the morning, all more than they ever said.
Of the new dead, that friend who died today,
Angel of suicides, gather him in now.
Defend us from doing what he had to do
Who threw himself away.

"Long Enough"

"Long enough. Long enough,"
I heard a woman say—
I am that woman who too long
Under the web lay.
Long enough in the empire
Of his darkened eyes
Bewildered in the greying silver
Light of his fantasies.

I have been lying here too long,
From shadow-begin to shadow-began
Where stretches over me the subtle
Rule of the Floating Man.
A young man and an old-young woman
May dive in the river between
And rise, the children of another country;
That riverbank, that green.

But too long, too long, too long
Is the journey through the ice
And too secret are the entrances
To my stretched hidingplace.
Walk out of the pudorweb
And into a lifetime
Said the woman; and I sleeper began to wake
And to say my own name.

Pouring Milk Away

Here, again. A smell of dying in the milk-pale carton,
And nothing then but pour the milk away.
More of the small and killed, the child's, wasted,
Little white arch of the drink and taste of day.
Spoiled, gone and forgotten; thrown away.

Day after day I do what I condemned in countries.
Look, the horror, the waste of food and bone.
You will know why when you have lived alone.

The Sixth Night: Waking

That first green night of their dreaming, asleep beneath
    the Tree,
God said, "Let meanings move," and there was poetry.

Waterlily Fire

for Richard Griffith

I. The Burning

Girl grown woman   fire   mother of fire
I go to the stone street turning to fire.   Voices
Go screaming   Fire   to the green glass wall.
And there where my youth flies blazing into fire
The   dance   of sane and insane images, noon
Of seasons and days.   Noontime of my one hour.

Saw down the bright noon street the crooked faces
Among the tall daylight in the city of change.
The scene has walls   stone   glass   all my gone life
One wall a web through which the moment walks
And I am open, and the opened hour
The world as water-garden   lying behind it.
In a city of stone, necessity of fountains,
Forced water fallen on glass, men with their axes.

An arm of flame reaches from water-green glass,
Behind the wall I know waterlilies
Drinking their light, transforming light and our eyes
Skythrown under water, clouds under those flowers,
Walls standing on all things stand in a city noon

Who will not believe a waterlily fire.
Whatever can happen in a city of stone,
Whatever can come to a wall can come to this wall.

I walk in the river of crisis toward the real,
I pass guards, finding the center of my fear
And you, Dick, endlessly my friend during storm.

The arm of flame striking through the wall of form.

II. The Island

Born of this river and this rock island, I relate
The changes   :   I born when the whirling snow
Rained past the general's grave and the amiable child
White past the windows of the house of Gyp the Blood.
General, gangster, child.   I know in myself the island.

I was the island without bridges, the child down whose
    blazing
Eye the men of plumes and bone raced their canoes and
    fire
Among the building of my young childhood, houses;
I was those changes, the live darknesses
Of wood, the pale grain of a grove in the fields
Over the river fronting red cliffs across   —
And always surrounding her the river, birdcries, the wild
Father building his sand, the mother in panic her
    parks   —
Bridges were thrown across, the girl arose
From sleeping streams of change in the change city.

The violent forgetting, the naked sides of darkness.
Fountain of a city in growth, an island of light and
    water.
Snow striking up past the graves, the yellow cry of
    spring.

Whatever can come to a city can come to this city.
Under the tall compulsion
                    of the past
I see the city
           change like a man changing
I love this man
               with my lifelong body of love
I know you
         among your changes
                    wherever I go
Hearing the sounds of building
                   the syllables of wrecking
A young girl watching
             the man throwing red hot rivets
Coals in a bucket of change
How can you love a city that will not stay?
I love you
        like a man of life in change.

Leaves like yesterday shed, the yellow of green spring
Like today accepted and become one's self
I go, I am a city with bridges and tunnels,
Rock, cloud, ships, voices.   To the man where the river
    met

The tracks, now buried deep along the Drive
Where blossoms like sex pink, dense pink, rose, pink,
        red.

Towers falling.   A dream of towers.
Necessity of fountains.   And my poor,
Stirring among our dreams,
Poor of my own spirit, and tribes, hope of towers
And lives, looking out through my eyes.
The city the growing body of our hate and love,
The root of the soul, and war in its black doorways.
A male sustained cry interrupting nightmare.
Male flower heading upstream.

Among a city of light, the stone that grows.
Stigma of dead stone, inert water, the tattered
Monuments rivetted against flesh.
Blue noon where the wall made big agonized men
Stand like sailors pinned howling on their lines, and I
See stopped in time a crime behind green glass,
Lilies of all my life on fire.
Flash faith in a city building its fantasies.

I walk past the guards into my city of change.

III. Journey Changes

Many of us   Each in his own life waiting
Waiting to move   Beginning to move   Walking
And early on the road of the hill of the world
Come to my landscapes emerging on the grass

The stages of the theatre of the journey

I see the time of willingness between plays
Waiting and walking and the play of the body
Silver body with its bosses and places
One by one touched awakened into into

Touched and turned one by one into   flame

The theatre of the advancing goddess   Blossoming
Smiles as she stands intensely being in stillness
Slowness in her blue dress advancing standing I go
And far across a field over the jewel grass

The play of the family stroke by stroke acted out

Gestures of deep acknowledging on the journey stages
Of the playings the play of the goddess and the god
A supple god of searching and reaching
Who weaves his strength   Who dances her more alive

The theatre of all animals, my snakes, my great horses

Always the journey   long   patient   many haltings
Many waitings for choice and again easy breathing
When the decision to go on is made
Along the long slopes of choice and again the world

The play of poetry approaching in its solving

Solvings of relations in poems and silences
For we were born to express   born for a journey
Caves, theatres, the companioned solitary way
And then I came to the place of mournful labor

A turn in the road and the long sight from the cliff

Over the scene of the land dug away to nothing and
        many
Seen to a stripped horizon carrying barrows of earth
A hod of earth taken and emptied and thrown away
Repeated farther than sight.   The voice saying slowly

But it is hell.   I heard my own voice in the words
Or it could be a foundation   And after the words
My chance came.   To enter.   The theatres of the
        world.

IV. Fragile

I think of the image brought into my room
Of the sage and the thin young man who flickers and
        asks.
He is asking about the moment when the Buddha
Offers the lotus, a flower held out as declaration.
"Isn't that fragile?" he asks.   The sage answers:
"I speak to you.   You speak to me.   Is that fragile?"

V. The Long Body

This journey is exploring us. Where the child stood
An island in a river of crisis, now
The bridges bind us in symbol, the sea
Is a bond, the sky reaches into our bodies.
We pray : we dive into each other's eyes.

Whatever can come to a woman can come to me.

This is the long body   :   into life from the beginning,
Big-headed infant unfolding into child, who stretches
        and finds
And then flowing the young one going tall, sunward,
And now full-grown, held, tense, setting feet to the
        ground,
Going as we go in the changes of the body,
As it is changes, in the long strip of our many
Shapes, as we range shifting through time.
The long body   :   a procession of images.

This moment in a city, in its dream of war.
                    We chose to be,
Becoming the only ones under the trees
                            when the harsh sound
Of the machine sirens spoke. There were these two
        men,
And the bearded one, the boys, the Negro mother
        feeding
Her baby. And threats, the ambulances with open doors.

Now silence. Everyone else within the walls. We sang.
                    We are the living island,
We the flesh of this island, being lived,
Whoever knows us is part of us today.

Whatever can happen to anyone can happen to me.

Fire striking its word among us, waterlilies
Reaching from darkness upward to a sun
Of rebirth, the implacable.   And in our myth
The Changing Woman who is still and who offers.

Eyes drinking light, transforming light, this day
That struggles with itself, brings itself to birth.
In ways of being, through silence, sources of light
Arriving behind my eye, a dialogue of light.

And everything a witness of the buried life.
This moment flowing across the sun, this force
Of flowers and voices body in body through space.
The city of endless cycles of the sun.

I speak to you   You speak to me

The Poem as Mask

Orpheus

When I wrote of the women in their dances and
　　wildness, it was a mask,
on their mountain, gold-hunting, singing, in orgy,
it was a mask; when I wrote of the god,
fragmented, exiled from himself, his life, the love gone
　　down with song,
it was myself, split open, unable to speak, in exile from
　　myself.

There is no mountain, there is no god, there is memory
of my torn life, myself split open in sleep, the rescued
　　child
beside me among the doctors, and a word
of rescue from the great eyes.

No more masks! No more mythologies!

Now, for the first time, the god lifts his hand,
the fragments join in me with their own music.

The Conjugation of the Paramecium

This has nothing
to do with
propagating

The species
is continued
as so many are
(among the smaller creatures)
by fission

(and this species
is very small
next in order to
the amoeba, the beginning one)

The paramecium
achieves, then,
immortality
by dividing

But when
the paramecium
desires renewal
strength   another joy
this is what
the paramecium does:

The paramecium
lies down beside
another
paramecium

Slowly   inexplicably
the exchange
takes place
in which
some bits
of the nucleus of each
are exchanged

for some bits
of the nucleus
of the other

This is called
the conjugation of the paramecium.

Double Dialogue

Homage to Robert Frost

In agony saying :   "The last night of his life,
My son and I in the kitchen   :   At half-past one
He said, 'I have failed as a husband. Now my wife
Is ill again and suffering.' At two
He said, 'I have failed as a farmer, for the sun
Is never there, the rain is never there.'
At three he said, 'I have failed as a poet who
Has never not once found my listener.
There is no sense to my life.' But then he heard me out.
I argued point by point. Seemed to win. Won.
He spoke to me once more when I was done:

'Even in argument, father, I have lost.'
He went and shot himself. Now tell me this one thing:
Should I have let him win then? Was I wrong?"

To answer for the land for love for song
Arguing life for life even at your life's cost.

Orgy

There were three of them that night.
They wanted it to happen in the first woman's room.
The man called her; the phone rang high.
Then she put fresh lipstick on.
Pretty soon he rang the bell.
She dreamed, she dreamed, she dreamed.
She scarcely looked him in the face
But gently took him to his place.
And after that the bell, the bell.
They looked each other in the eyes,
A hot July it was that night,
And he then slow took off his tie,
And she then slow took off her scarf,
The second one took off her scarf,
And he then slow his heavy shoe,
And she then slow took off her shoe,
The other one took off her shoe,
He then took off his other shoe,
The second one, her other shoe,
A hot July it was that night.

And he then slow took off his belt,
And she then slow took off her belt,
The second one took off her belt . . .

What I See

Lie there, in sweat and dream, I do, and "there"
Is here, my bed, on which I dream
You, lying there, on yours, locked, pouring love,
While I tormented here see in my reins
You, perfectly at climax. And the lion strikes.
I want you with whatever obsessions come—
I wanted your obsession to be mine
But if it is that unknown half-suggested strange
Other figure locked in your climax, then
I here, I want you and the other, want your obsession,
    want
Whatever is locked into you now while I sweat and
    dream.

Gift

the child, the poems, the child, the poems, the journeys
    back and forth across our long country
        of opposites,
and through myself, through you, away from you, toward
    you, the dreams of madness and of an
        impossible complete time—
gift be forgiven.

Cries from Chiapas

Hunger
> of mountains
>> spoke
>>> from a tiger's throat.

Tiger-tooth peaks.
> The moon.
>> A thousand mists

turning.
> Desires of mountains
>> like the desires of women,

moon-drawn,
> distant,
>> clear black among
>>> confusions of silver.

Women of Chiapas!
> Dream-borne
>> voices of women.

Splinters of mountains,
> broken obsidian,
>> silver.

White tigers
> haunting
>> your forehead here
>>> sloped in shadow—

black hungers of women,
> confusion
>> turning like tigers

And your voice—

I am
    almost asleep
        almost awake
            in your arms.

For My Son

You come from poets, kings, bankrupts, preachers,
    attempted bankrupts, builders of cities, salesmen,
the great rabbis, the kings of Ireland, failed drygoods
    storekeepers, beautiful women of the songs,
great horsemen, tyrannical fathers at the shore of ocean,
    the western mothers looking west beyond from
    their windows,
the families escaping over the sea hurriedly and by
    night—
the roundtowers of the Celtic violet sunset,
the diseased, the radiant, fliers, men thrown out of
    town, the man bribed by his cousins to stay out of
    town, teachers, the cantor on Friday evening, the
    lurid newspapers,
strong women gracefully holding relationship, the
    Jewish girl going to parochial school, the boys
    racing their iceboats on the Lakes,
the woman still before the diamond in the velvet
    window, saying "Wonder of nature."

Like all men,
you come from singers, the ghettoes, the famines, wars
     and refusal of wars, men who built villages
that grew to our solar cities, students, revolutionists, the
     pouring of buildings, the market newspapers,
a poor tailor in a darkening room,
a wilderness man, the hero of mines, the astronomer, a
     white-faced woman hour on hour teaching piano
     and her crippled wrist,
like all men,
you have not seen your father's face
but he is known to you forever in song, the coast of the
     skies, in dream, wherever you find man play playing
     his part as father, father among our light, among
     our darkness,
and in your self made whole, whole with yourself and
     whole with others,
the stars your ancestors.

Poem

I lived in the first century of world wars.
Most mornings I would be more or less insane,
The newspapers would arrive with their careless stories,
The news would pour out of various devices
Interrupted by attempts to sell products to the unseen.
I would call my friends on other devices;
They would be more or less mad for similar reasons.
Slowly I would get to pen and paper,
Make my poems for others unseen and unborn.

In the day I would be reminded of those men and
      women
Brave, setting up signals across vast distances,
Considering a nameless way of living, of almost unimag-
      ined values.
As the lights darkened, as the lights of night brightened,
We would try to imagine them, try to find each other.
To construct peace, to make love, to reconcile
Waking with sleeping, ourselves with each other,
Ourselves with ourselves. We would try by any means
To reach the limits of ourselves, to reach beyond
      ourselves,
To let go the means, to wake.

I lived in the first century of these wars.

The Power of Suicide

The potflower on the windowsill says to me
In words that are green-edged red leaves   :
Flower   flower   flower   flower
Today for the sake of all the dead   Burst into flower.

(1963)

Bunk Johnson Blowing

in memory of Leadbelly
and his house on 59th Street

They found him in the fields and called him back to
    music.
Can't, he said, my teeth are gone.   They bought him
    teeth.

Bunk Johnson's trumpet on a California
early May evening, calling me to
breath of . . .
up those stairs . . .
calling me to
look into
the face of that
trumpet
experience
and past it
his eyes

Jim and Rita beside me. We drank it. Jim had just come
    back
from Sacramento the houses made of piano boxes the
    bar without
a sign and the Mexicans drinking we drank the trumpet
    music
and drank that black park moonlit beneath the willow
    trees,
Bunk Johnson blowing all night out of that full moon.
Two-towered church. Rita listening to it, all night
music! said, I'm supposed to, despise them.

Tears streaming down her face. Said, don't tell my
    ancestors.

We three slid down that San Francisco hill.

What They Said

:   After I am dead, darling,
            my seventeen senses gone,
        I shall love you as you wish,
            no sex, no mouth, but bone—
            in the way you long for now,
        with my soul alone.

:   When we are neither woman nor man
            but bleached to skeleton—
        when you have changed, my darling,
            and all your senses gone,
            it is not me that you will love:
        you will love everyone.

The Backside of the Academy

Five brick panels, three small windows, six lions' heads
    with rings in their mouths, five pairs of closed
    bronze doors—
the shut wall with the words carved across its head
ART REMAINS THE ONE WAY POSSIBLE OF
    SPEAKING TRUTH.—

On this May morning, light swimming in this street, the
    children running,
on the church beside the Academy the lines are flying
of little yellow-and-white plastic flags flapping in the
    light;
and on the great shut wall, the words are carved across:
WE ARE YOUNG AND WE ARE FRIENDS OF
    TIME.—
Below that, a light blue asterisk in chalk
and in white chalk, Hector, Joey, Lynn, Rudolfo.
A little up the street, a woman shakes a small dark boy,
she shouts What's wrong with you, ringing that bell!
In the street of rape and singing, poems, small
    robberies,
carved in an oblong panel of the stone:
CONSCIOUS UTTERANCE OF THOUGHT BY
    SPEECH OR ACTION
TO ANY END IS ART.—
On the lowest reach of the walls are chalked the words:
    Jack is a object,
Walter and Trina, Goo Goo, I love Trina,
and further along Viva Fidel now altered to Muera
    Fidel.
A deep blue marble is lodged against the curb.
A phone booth on one corner; on the other, the big
    mesh basket for trash.
Beyond them, the little park is always locked. For the
    two soldier brothers.
And past that goes on an eternal football game
which sometimes, as on this day in May, transforms to
    stickball

as, for one day in May,
five pairs of closed bronze doors will open
and the Academy of writers, sculptors, painters,
     composers, their guests and publishers will all roll
     in and
the wave of organ music come rolling out into
the street where light now blows and papers and little
     children and words, some breezes of Spanish blow
     and many colors of people.
A watch cap lies fallen against a cellophane which used
     to hold pistachio nuts
and here before me, on my street,
five brick panels, three small windows, six lions' heads
     with rings in their mouths, five pairs of closed
     bronze doors,
light flooding the street I live and write in; and across
     the river the one word FREE against the ferris
     wheel and the roller coaster,
and here, painted upon the stones, Chino, Bobby, Joey,
     Fatmoma, Willy, Holy of God
and also Margaret is a shit and also fuck and shit;
far up, invisible at the side of the building:
WITHOUT VISION THE PEO
and on the other side, the church side,
where shadows of trees and branches, this day in May,
     are printed balanced on the church wall,
in-focus trunks and softened-focus branches
below the roof where the two structures stand,
bell and cross, antenna and weathervane,
I can see past the church the words of an ending line:
IVE BY BREAD ALONE.

The Outer Banks

I

Horizon of islands shifting
Sea-light flame on my voice
                              burn in me
                                        Light
flows from the water from sands   islands of this
        horizon
The sea comes toward me across the sea.   The sand
moves over the sand in waves
between the guardians of this landscape
the great commemorative statue on one hand
        —the first flight of man, outside of dream,
                seen as stone wing and stainless steel—
and at the other hand
        banded black-and-white, climbing
the spiral lighthouse.

Note: This country, the Outer Banks of North Carolina, is a strong
    country of imagination: Raleigh's first settlements, in which
    Thomas Hariot the scientist served a year in the New World, were
    here; the Wright Brothers flew from here; Hart Crane's "Hatteras"
    is set among these sand-bars, these waters. Several journeys here,
    the last one for the sake of the traces of Thomas Hariot (toward a
    biography I was writing) led me to this poem. The *Tiger*, in the last
    part of the poem, is one of the ships sent out by Raleigh. The quota-
    tions are from Selma, Alabama, in 1965. The truncated wing is a
    monument to the Wright Brothers. The spiral lighthouse is Hat-
    teras light.

II

Flood over ocean,
avalanche on the flat beach. Pouring.
Indians holding branches up, to
placate the tempest,
the one-legged twisting god that is
a standing wind.
Rays are branching from all things:
great serpent, great plume, constellation:
sands from which colors and light pass,
the lives of plants.   Animals.   Men.
A man and a woman reach for each other.

III

Wave of the sea.

IV

Sands have washed, sea has flown over us.
Between the two guardians, spiral, truncated wing,
history and these wild birds
Bird-voiced discoverers :   Hariot,   Hart Crane,
the brothers who watched gulls.
"No bird soars in a calm,"   said Wilbur Wright.
Dragon of the winds forms over me.
Your dance, goddesses in your circle
sea-wreath, whirling of the event
behind me on land as deep in our own lives
we begin to know the movement to come.
Sunken, drowned spirals,
hurricane-dance.

V

Shifting of islands on this horizon.
The cycle of changes in the Book of Changes.
Two islands making an open female line.
That powerful long straight bar a male island.
The building of the surf
constructing immensities
between the pale flat Sound
and ocean ever
birds as before earthquake
winds fly from all origins
the length of this wave goes from the great wing
down coast, the barrier beach in all its miles
road of the sun and the moon to
a spiral lighthouse
to the depth turbulence
lifts up its wave like cities
the ocean in the air
spills down the world.

VI

A man is walking toward me across the water.
From far out, the flat waters of the Sound,
he walks pulling his small boat

In the shoal water.

A man who is white and has been fishing.
Walks steadily upon the light of day
Coming closer to me where I stand
looking into the sun and the blaze inner water.

Clear factual surface over which he pulls
a boat over a closing quarter-mile.

VII

Speak to it, says the light.
Speak to it music,
voices of the sea and human throats.
Origins of spirals,
the ballad and original sweet grape
dark on the vines near Hatteras,
tendrils of those vines, whose spiral tower
now rears its light, accompanying
all my voices.

VIII

He walks toward me.   A black man in the sun.
He now is a black man speaking to my heart
crisis of darkness in this century
of moments of this speech.

The boat is slowly nearer drawn, this man.

The zigzag power coming straight, in stones,
        in arcs, metal, crystal, the spiral
in sacred wet
                schematic elements of
cities, music, arrangement
spin these stones of home
                        under the sea
return to the stations of the stars
and the sea, speaking across its lives.

A man who is bones is close to me
drawing a boat of bones
the sun behind him
is another color of fire,
the sea behind me
rears its flame.

A man whose body flames and tapers in flame
twisted tines of remembrance that dissolve
a pitchfork of the land worn thin
flame up and dissolve again

                          draw   small   boat

Nets of the stars at sunset over us.
This draws me home to the home of the wild birds
long-throated birds of this passage.
This is the edge of experience, *grenzen der seele*
where those on the verge of human understanding
the borderline people stand on the shifting islands
among the drowned stars and the tempest.
"Everyman's mind, like the dumbest,
claws at his own furthest limits of knowing the world,"
a man in a locked room said.

Open to the sky
I stand before this boat that looks at me.
The man's flames are arms and legs.
Body, eye, head, stars, sands look at me.

I walk out into the shoal water
and throw my leg over the wall of the boat.

         x

At one shock, speechlessness.
I am in the bow, on the short thwart.
He is standing before me amidships, rowing forward
like my old northern sea-captain in his dory.
All things have spun.
The words gone,
I facing sternwards, looking at the gate
between the barrier islands.   As he rows.
Sand islands shifting and the last of land
a pale and open line   horizon
sea.

With whose face did he look at me?
What did I say?   or did I say?
in speechlessness
move to the change.
These strokes provide the music,
and the accused boy on land today saying
What did I say?   or did I say?
The dream on land last night built this the boat of death
but in the suffering of the light
moving across the sea
do we in our moving
move toward life or death

Hurricane, skullface, the sky's size
winds streaming through his teeth
doing the madman's twist

and not a beach not flooded

nevertheless, here
stability of light
my other silence
and at my left hand and at my right hand
no longer wing and lighthouse
no longer the guardians.
They are in me, in my speechless
life of barrier beach.
As it lies open
to the night, out there.

Now seeing my death before me
starting again, among the drowned men,
desperate men, unprotected discoverers,
and the man before me
here.
Stroke by stroke drawing us.
Out there? Father of rhythms,
deep wave, mother.
There is no *out there*.
All is open.
Open water. Open I.

The wreck of the *Tiger*, the early pirate, the blood-
    clam's ark, the tern's acute eye, all buried mathe-
    matical instruments, castaways, pelicans, drowned
    five-strand pearl necklaces, hopes of livelihood,
    hopes of grace,
walls of houses, sepia sea-fences, the writhen octopus
    and those tall masts and sails,
marked hulls of ships and last month's plane, dipping his
    salute to the stone wing of dream,
turbulence, Diamond Shoals, the dark young living
    people:
"Sing one more song and you are under arrest."
"Sing another song."
Women, ships, lost voices.
Whatever has dissolved into our waves.
I a lost voice
moving, calling you
on the edge of the moment that is now the center.
From the open sea.

Käthe Kollwitz

I

Held between wars
my lifetime
    among wars, the big hands of the world of death
my lifetime
listens to yours.

The faces of the sufferers
in the street, in dailiness,
their lives showing
through their bodies
a look as of music
the revolutionary look
that says   I am in the world
to change the world
my lifetime
is to love to endure to suffer the music
to set its portrait
up as a sheet of the world
the most moving the most alive
Easter and bone
and Faust walking among the flowers of the world
and the child alive within the living woman, music of
         man,
and death holding my lifetime between great hands
the hands of enduring life
that suffers the gifts and madness of full life, on earth, in
         our time,
and through my life, through my eyes, through my arms
         and hands
may give the face of this music in portrait waiting for
the unknown person
held in the two hands, you.

II

Woman as gates, saying   :
"The process is after all like music,

like the development of a piece of music.
The fugues come back and
                                again and again
interweave.
A theme may seem to have been put aside,
but it keeps returning—
the same thing modulated,
somewhat changed in form.
Usually richer.
And it is very good that this is so."

A woman pouring her opposites.
"After all there are happy things in life too.
Why do you show only the dark side?"
"I could not answer this. But I know—
in the beginning my impulse to know
the working life
                had little to do with
pity or sympathy.
                I simply felt
that the life of the workers was beautiful."

She said, "I am groping in the dark."

She said, "When the door opens, of sensuality,
then you will understand it too. The struggle begins.
Never again to be free of it,
often you will feel it to be your enemy.
Sometimes
you will almost suffocate,
such joy it brings."

Saying of her husband : "My wish
is to die after Karl.
I know no person who can love as he can,
with his whole soul.
Often this love has oppressed me;
I wanted to be free.
But often too it has made me
so terribly happy."

She said : "We rowed over to Carrara at dawn,
climbed up to the marble quarries
and rowed back at night. The drops of water
fell like glittering stars
from our oars."

She said: "As a matter of fact,
I believe
        that bisexuality
is almost   a necessary factor
in artistic production; at any rate,
the tinge of masculinity within me
helped me
        in my work."

She said : "The only technique I can still manage.
It's hardly a technique at all, lithography.
In it
    only the essentials count."

A tight-lipped man in a restaurant last night saying to
    me :
"Kollwitz?   She's too black-and-white."

III

Held among wars, watching
   all of them
   all these people
   weavers,
   Carmagnole

Looking at
   all of them
   death, the children
   patients in waiting-rooms
   famine
   the street
   the corpse with the baby
   floating, on the dark river

A woman seeing
   the violent, inexorable
   movement of nakedness
   and the confession of No
   the confession of great weakness, war,
   all streaming to one son killed, Peter;
   even the son left living; repeated,
   the father, the mother; the grandson
   another Peter killed in another war; firestorm;
   dark, light, as two hands,
   this pole and that pole as the gates.

What would happen if one woman told the truth about
   her life?
   The world would split open

IV. Song : The Calling-Up

Rumor, stir of ripeness
rising within the girl
sensual blossoming
of meaning, its light and form.

The birth-cry summoning
out of the male, the father
from the warm woman
a mother in response.

The word of death
calls up the fight with stone
wrestle with grief with time
from the material make
an art harder than bronze.

V. Self-Portrait

Mouth looking directly at you
eyes in their inwardness looking
directly at you
half light   half darkness
woman, strong, German, young artist
flows into
wide sensual mouth meditating
looking right at you
eyes shadowed with brave hand
looking deep at you
flows into
wounded brave mouth

grieving and hooded eyes
alive, German, in her first War
flows into
strength of the worn face
a skein of lines
broods, flows into
mothers among the war graves
bent over death
facing the father
stubborn upon the field
flows into
the marks of her knowing—
Nie Wieder Krieg
repeated in the eyes
flows into
"Seedcorn must not be ground"
and the grooved cheek
lips drawn fine
the down-drawn grief
face of our age
flows into
Pieta, mother and
between her knees
life as her son in death
pouring from the sky of
one more war
flows into
face almost obliterated
hand over the mouth forever
hand over one eye now
the other great eye
closed

Despisals

In the human cities, never again to
despise the backside of the city, the ghetto,
or build it again as we build the despised
backsides of houses.   Look at your own building.
You are the city.

Among our secrecies, not to despise our Jews
(that is, ourselves) or our darkness, our blacks,
or in our sexuality   wherever it takes us
and we now know we are productive
too productive, too reproductive
for our present invention — never to despise
the homosexual who goes building another

with touch   with touch   (not to despise any touch)
each like himself, like herself each.
You are this.

In the body's ghetto
never to go despising the asshole
nor the useful shit that is our clean clue
to what we need.   Never to despise
the clitoris in her least speech.

Never to despise in myself what I have been taught
to despise.   Nor to despise the other.
Not to despise the *it*.   To make this relation
with the it   :   to know that I am it.

Looking at Each Other

Yes, we were looking at each other
Yes, we knew each other very well
Yes, we had made love with each other many times
Yes, we had heard music together
Yes, we had gone to the sea together
Yes, we had cooked and eaten together
Yes, we had laughed often day and night
Yes, we fought violence and knew violence
Yes, we hated the inner and outer oppression
Yes, that day we were looking at each other
Yes, we saw the sunlight pouring down
Yes, the corner of the table was between us
Yes, bread and flowers were on the table
Yes, our eyes saw each other's eyes
Yes, our mouths saw each other's mouths
Yes, our breasts saw each other's breasts
Yes, our bodies entire saw each other
Yes, it was beginning in each
Yes, it threw waves across our lives
Yes, the pulses were becoming very strong
Yes, the beating became very delicate
Yes, the calling   the arousal

Yes, the arriving   the coming
Yes, there it was for both entire
Yes, we were looking at each other

Waiting for Icarus

He said he would be back and we'd drink wine together
He said that everything would be better than before
He said we were on the edge of a new relation
He said he would never again cringe before his father
He said that he was going to invent full-time
He said he loved me that going into me
He said was going into the world and the sky
He said all the buckles were very firm
He said the wax was the best wax
He said Wait for me here on the beach
He said Just don't cry

I remember the gulls and the waves
I remember the islands going dark on the sea
I remember the girls laughing
I remember they said he only wanted to get away from
        me
I remember mother saying   :   Inventors are like poets,
                                            a trashy lot
I remember she told me those who try out inventions
        are worse
I remember she added   :   Women who love such are
        the worst of all

I have been waiting all day, or perhaps longer.
I would have liked to try those wings myself.
It would have been better than this.

In Her Burning

The randy old
woman said
Tickle me up
I'll be
dead very soon—
Nothing will
touch me then
but the clouds
of the sky
and the bone-
white light
off the moon
Touch me
before I go
down
among the bones
My dear one
alone
to the night—
I said
I know I know
But all I know
tonight
Is that the sun

and the moon
they burn
with the one
one light.

In her burning
signing
what does the
white moon say?
The moon says
The sun
is shining.

Myth

Long afterward, Oedipus, old and blinded, walked the
roads.   He smelled a familiar smell.   It was
the Sphinx.   Oedipus said, "I want to ask one question.
Why didn't I recognize my mother?"   "You gave the
wrong answer," said the Sphinx.   "But that was what
made everything possible," said Oedipus.   "No," she
        said.
"When I asked, What walks on four legs in the
        morning,
two at noon, and three in the evening, you answered,
Man.   You didn't say anything about woman."
"When you say Man," said Oedipus, "you include
        women
too. Everyone knows that."   She said, "That's what
you think."

A Simple Experiment

When a magnet is
struck by a hammer
the magnetism spills out of
the iron.

The molecules
are jarred,
they are a mob going
in all directions

The magnet is
shockéd back
it is no magnet but
simple iron.

There is no more
of its former
kind of accord
or force.

But if you take
another magnet
and stroke the iron
with this,

it can be
remagnetized
if you stroke it
and stroke it,

stroke it
stroke it,
the molecules
can be given
their tending grace

by a strong magnet
stroking stroking
always in the same direction,
of course.

Ballad of Orange and Grape

After you finish your work
after you do your day
after you've read your reading
after you've written your say   —
you go down the street to the hot dog stand,
one block down and across the way.
On a blistering afternoon in East Harlem in the
        twentieth century.

Most of the windows are boarded up,
the rats run out of a sack   —
sticking out of the crummy garage
one shiny long Cadillac;
at the glass door of the drug-addiction center,
a man who'd like to break your back.
But here's a brown woman with a little girl dressed in
        rose and pink, too.

Frankfurters frankfurters sizzle on the steel
where the hot-dog-man leans   —
nothing else on the counter
but the usual two machines,
the grape one, empty, and the orange one, empty,
I face him in between.
A black boy comes along, looks at the hot dogs, goes on
     walking.

I watch the man as he stands and pours
in the familiar shape
bright purple in the one marked ORANGE
orange in the one marked GRAPE,
the grape drink in the machine marked ORANGE
and orange drink in the GRAPE.
Just the one word large and clear, unmistakable, on each
     machine.

I ask him   :   How can we go on reading
and make sense out of what we read?   —
How can they write and believe what they're writing,
the young ones across the street,
while you go on pouring grape into ORANGE
and orange into the one marked GRAPE   —?
(How are we going to believe what we read and we
     write and we hear and we say and we do?)

He looks at the two machines and he smiles
and he shrugs and smiles and pours again.
It could be violence and nonviolence
it could be white and black   women and men

it could be war and peace or any
binary system, love and hate, enemy, friend.
Yes and no, be and not-be, what we do and what we
     don't do.

On a corner in East Harlem
garbage, reading, a deep smile, rape,
forgetfulness, a hot street of murder,
misery, withered hope,
a man keeps pouring grape into ORANGE
and orange into the one marked GRAPE,
pouring orange into GRAPE and grape into ORANGE
     forever.

From a Play : Publisher's Song

I lie in the bath and I contemplate the toilet-paper:
Scottissue, 1000 sheets   —
     What a lot of pissin and shittin,
     What a lot of pissin and shittin,
Enough for the poems of Shelley and Keats   —
All the poems of Shelley and Keats.

St. Roach

For that I never knew you, I only learned to dread you,
for that I never touched you, they told me you are filth,
they showed me by every action to despise your kind;
for that I saw my people making war on you,
I could not tell you apart, one from another,
for that in childhood I lived in places clear of you,
for that all the people I knew met you by
crushing you, stamping you to death, they poured
     boiling water on you, they flushed you down,
for that I could not tell one from another
only that you were dark, fast on your feet, and slender.
     Not like me.
For that I did not know your poems
And that I do not know any of your sayings
And that I cannot speak or read your language
And that I do not sing your songs
And that I do not teach our children
     to eat your food
     or know your poems
     or sing your songs
But that we say you are filthing our food
But that we know you not at all.

Yesterday I looked at one of you for the first time.
You were lighter than the others in color, that was
    neither good nor bad.
I was really looking for the first time.
You seemed troubled and witty.

Today I touched one of you for the first time.
You were startled, you ran, you fled away
Fast as a dancer, light, strange and lovely to the touch.
I reach, I touch, I begin to know you.

Painters

In the cave with a long-ago flare
a woman stands, her arm up. Red twig, black twig,
    brown twig.
A wall of leaping darkness over her.
The men are out hunting in the early light
But here in this flicker, one or two men, painting
and a woman among them.
Great living animals grow on the stone walls,
their pelts, their eyes, their sex, their hearts,
and the cave-painters touch them with life, red, brown,
    black,
a woman among them, painting.

Ms. Lot

Well, if he treats me like a young girl still,
That father of mine, and here's my sister
And we're still traveling into the hills—
But everyone on the road knows he offered us
To the Strangers when all they wanted was men,
And the cloud of smoke still over the twin cities
And mother a salt lick the animals come to—
Who's going to want me now?
Mother did not even know
She was not to turn around and look.
God spoke to Lot, my father.
She was hard of hearing.   He knew that.
I don't believe he told her, anyway.
What kind of father is that, or husband?
He offered us to those men.   They didn't want women.
Mother always used to say:
Some normal man will come along and need you.

Resurrection of the Right Side

When the half-body dies its frightful death
forked pain, infection of snakes, lightning, pull down
     the voice.   Waking
and I begin to climb the mountain on my mouth,
word by stammer, walk stammered, the lurching deck of
     earth.
Left-right with none of my own rhythms

the long-established sex and poetry.

> I go running in sleep,

but waking stumble down corridors of self, all rhythms
    gone.

The broken movement of love   sex out of rhythm
one halted name   in a shattered language
ruin of French-blue lights behind the eyes
slowly the left hand extends a hundred feet
and the right hand follows follows
but still the power of sight is very weak
but I go rolling this ball of life, it rolls
and I follow it whole up the slowly-brightening slope

A whisper attempts me, I whisper without stammer
I walk the long hall to the time of a metronome
set by a child's gun-target   left-right
the power of eyesight is very slowly arriving
      in this late impossible daybreak
      all the blue flowers open

The Wards

St. George's Hospital,
Hyde Park Corner

Lying in the moment, she climbs white snows;
At the foot of the bed the chart relates.
Here a man burns in fever; he is here, he is there,
Five thousand years ago in the cave country.

In this bed, I go wandering in Macao,
I run all night the black alleys.   Time runs
Over the edge and all exists in all.   We hold
All human history, all geography,
I cannot remember the word for what I need.
Our explorations, all at the precipice,
The night-table, a landscape of zebras,
Transistor constellations.   All this music,
I heard it forming before I was born.   I come
In this way, to the place.
                          Our selves lit clear,
This moment giving me necessity
Gives us ourselves and we risk everything,
Walking into our life.

Destruction of Grief

Today I asked Aileen
at the Film Library to help me find
those girl twins of the long-gone summer.
Aileen, who were they?
I was seven, the lion circus
was pitched in the field of sand and swordgrass
near the ocean, behind the Tackapoosha Garage.
The ancient land of the Waramaug Indians.
Now there's a summer hotel.
The first day of that circus dazzles me forever.
I stayed.   That evening
the police came looking for me.
Easy to find, behind

the bales of hay, with Caesar's tamer,
the clowns, and the girl twins.
My father and mother forgave me, for they loved
circuses, opera, carnivals, New York, popular songs.
All day that summer, all July and August,
I stayed behind the tents with the twin girls,
with Caesar the lion my friend,
with the lion-tamer.
Do you know their names, Aileen?
The girls went into the early movies.
Late August, Caesar mauled the man's right hand.
I want to remember the names of those twins.
You could see he would not ever keep his hand.
Smell of the ocean, straw,
lordly animal rankness, gunpowder.
"Yes, they destroyed Caesar," I was told that night.
Those twins became movie stars.
Those of us who were there that summer—
Joey killed himself, I saw Tommy
just before the war; is Henry around?
Helene is in real estate—and the twins—
can you tell me their names, Aileen?

Burnishing, Oakland

Near the waterfront
mouth of a wide shed   open
many-shining bronze flat
ship-propellors hanging in air
propellors lying blunt on ground

The vast sound and shine
screaming its word

One man masked
holding a heavy weight
on the end of a weighted boom
counterbalanced
I see him draw
his burnisher
along the bronze
high scream of burnishing
a path of brightness

Outside, the prowl cars
Oakland police
cruising past
behind them the trailing
Panther cars
to witness to
any encounter

Statement of light
I see as we drive past
act of light
among sleeping houses
in our need
the dark people

Behind my head
the shoulders of hills
and the dark houses.

Here in the shine, the singing cry
near the extreme
of the range of knowing
one masked man
working alone
burnishing

BIOGRAPHICAL NOTE

NOTE ON THE TEXTS

NOTES

INDEX OF TITLES &
FIRST LINES

BIOGRAPHICAL NOTE

Muriel Rukeyser was born on December 15, 1913, in New York City. The daughter of well-to-do Jewish parents, she attended the Ethical Culture and Fieldston schools in Manhattan, then enrolled at Vassar College in 1930. She took courses at Columbia College in the summers of 1931 and 1932. At Vassar, she founded (with Elizabeth Bishop, Mary McCarthy, and Eleanor Clark) the undergraduate journal *Student Review*, serving as literary editor. Covering the notorious Scottsboro case for the journal in 1933, she traveled to Alabama and was arrested and jailed because she discussed the case with African-American journalists. After leaving Vassar, she moved back to Manhattan. She took flying lessons in 1933 at Roosevelt Aviation School. In 1935, she was named associate editor of *New Theatre* magazine. Her debut collection *Theory of Flight* (1935) won the Yale Younger Poets Award. She visited West Virginia in 1936 to research the silicosis deaths among workers digging a tunnel for a hydroelectric project, an incident at the center of her long sequence of poems "The Book of the Dead." Reporting on the People's Olympiad, an athletic event organized in protest against the Olympics being held in Nazi Germany, she was in Spain at the outbreak of its civil war; after

her return to the U.S. she was an active supporter of the Span-
ish anti-Fascists. She taught at Sarah Lawrence College, first in
1946 and then from 1956 to 1967. She moved to San Francisco
in 1945, working as an instructor at the California Labor
School. Her son William was born in 1947. She returned to
New York City in 1954. She suffered a stroke in 1964 but con-
tinued to write. Actively opposed to the Vietnam War, she was
arrested at a protest on the steps of the U.S. Capitol; she trav-
eled to Hanoi with poet Denise Levertov in 1972. Three years
later, she visited Seoul on behalf of the jailed Korean poet Kim
Chi-Ha, who had been sentenced to death on charges of com-
munist conspiracy against the state. She was a member of the
National Institute of Arts and Letters and served as president
of the American Center of P.E.N., 1975–76. She died of a heart
attack on February 12, 1980.

Selected Bibliography

Tim Dalton, *Muriel Rukeyser's Book of the Dead*. Columbia: University of Missouri
    Press, 2003.
Kate Daniels and Richard Jones (eds.), *Poetry East: nos. 16 and 17: a special double
    issue on Muriel Rukeyser*. Charlottesville, Virginia: Spring / Summer 1985.
Suzanne Gardinier, *A World That Will Hold All the People*. Ann Arbor, University
    of Michigan Press, 1996.
Anne F. Herzog and Janet Kaufman (eds.), *How Shall We Tell Each Other of the
    Poet? The Life and Writing of Muriel Rukeyser*. Foreword by Alicia Suskin
    Ostriker. New York: St. Martin's Press, 1999.
Louise Kertesz, *The Poetic Vision of Muriel Rukeyser*. Foreword by Kenneth
    Rexroth. Baton Rouge and London: Louisiana State University Press, 1980.
Jan Heller Levi, ed., *A Muriel Rukeyser Reader*. Introduction by Adrienne Rich.
    New York: W. W. Norton & Co., 1994.
Muriel Rukeyser, *The Collected Poems*. New York: McGraw-Hill, 1978.
——. *Houdini: A Musical*. Ashfield MA: Paris Press, 2002.
——. *The Life of Poetry*. Foreword by Jane Cooper. Ashfield MA: Paris Press,
    1996 (William Morrow, 1949).
——. *The Orgy*. Foreword by Sharon Olds. Ashfield MA: Paris Press, 1997
    (Coward McCann, 1965).

NOTE ON THE TEXTS

With the exception of translations and children's verse, Rukeyser gathered all of her poetry published in book form since her first volume *Theory of Flight* (1935) in *The Collected Poems of Muriel Rukeyser* (New York: McGraw-Hill, 1978), from which the texts in the present volume are taken. For the most part Rukeyser did not revise her poems after they first appeared in book form. For *Selected Poems* (Norfolk, CT: New Directions, 1951), however, she made extensive cuts in several poems, such as "The Book of the Dead," presumably because of space limitations; most of the cut passages were restored in subsequent collections such as *Waterlily Fire: Poems 1935–1962* (New York: Macmillan, 1962) and *The Collected Poems*. Occasionally there are passages in which *The Collected Poems* versions differ from those in earlier book publications other than *Selected Poems*. The significant variants—such as the long version of "Darkness Music" or the final line, later cut, of "Reading Time : 1 Minute 26 Seconds"—are listed in the notes.

This volume corrects the following typographical errors in *The Collected Poems*, cited by page and line number: 9.24, Father!; 11.17, left.; 31.9, poeple; 33.24, sits.; 34.2, cheap,; 48.5, all; 60.20, them; 66.15, promised; 74.19, fact; 79.6, dream; 113.15, My; 125.11, This called; 134.29, and; 153.16, of; 156.13, you're; 161.26, rhythms.

NOTES

1.6   Not Angles, angels]   According to Bede's *Ecclesiastical History of England*, Gregory the Great (c. 540–604) inquired about some British children who were slaves in Rome. He was told, "They are Angles" (*sunt Angli*), to which he replied, "They are not Angles but angels" (*non Angli sed angeli*), and added that they would become Christians. Later as pope he sent missionaries to the British Isles.

1.20–22   Loeb . . . throat.]   On May 21, 1924, Nathan Leopold and Richard Loeb, two 19-year-olds from Chicago, murdered 14-year-old Bobby Franks, a distant relative of Loeb's. Their trial, in which they were represented by Clarence Darrow, resulted in convictions and life sentences for both. Sons of wealthy, respectable South Side families, both were attending the University of Chicago at the time of the murder; Leopold in particular was interested in philosophy, especially the ideas of Friedrich Nietzsche, whose "influence" on the killing was emphasized by Darrow in his defense and in press accounts of the trial.

2.10   Sacco]   Nicola Sacco (1891–1927), anarchist Italian immigrant who with Bartolomeo Vanzetti (1888–1927) was convicted of murder and armed robbery in 1920 and executed despite international protests that their guilt had not been proven.

2.18   Prinzip's year]   I.e., 1914, when Serbian student Gavrilo Princip assassinated Archduke Francis Ferdinand of Austria in Sarajevo and set in motion events that led to the outbreak of World War I.

11.15   Objectivist poet fresh from Butte]   The Objectivists, a group of poets whose work was collected in the February 1931 issue of *Poetry* magazine and in *An "Objectivists" Anthology* (Cagnes-sur-mer, France: To Press, 1932). Poets affiliated with the group included Louis Zukofsky, Charles Reznikoff, George Oppen, and Carl Rakosi, and later Lorine Neidecker and Basil Bunting. The "Objectivist poet from Butte" may also refer to Eli Siegel (1902–1978), poet whose "Hot Afternoons Have Been in Montana" won the *Nation* Poetry Prize in 1925, though Siegel was not associated with the Objectivist group.

25.4   The Book of the Dead]   In the late 1920s, the New Kanawha Power Company, a subsidiary of Union Carbide, hired the construction firm of Rinehart & Dennis to dig the Hawk's Nest Tunnel through a mountain at Gauley Bridge, West Virginia. Thousands of workers on the project were exposed to toxic silica dust, causing at least 700 people to die from silicosis. Articles in magazines such as *Time*, *Newsweek*, and *The Nation* prompted a national outcry over corporate negligence toward the tunnel workers that led to an investigation by the House of Representatives subcommittee on Labor. Much of "The Book of the Dead" is adapted from transcripts of the congressional inquiry. In a note in *Selected Poems* (1951) Rukeyser writes: "The twenty poems of *The Book of the Dead* present a valley in West Virginia—a steep river-gorge where a tunnel and dam had been built. Silica, almost pure, had been encountered in the rock. The men who worked there, under threat of illness and death because of the silica, and unprotected, were dying now; they were being fought over in the courts, by the doctors, and in Congress; the women and children in the valley had come into this primitive state of war, among the fierce colored landscape and the precise buildings of the dam and power-plant."

31.5   Gamoca . . . Alloy]   Towns near Gauley Bridge.

35.18   Mellon's]   Andrew Mellon (1855–1937), American financier.

38.16   Griswold]   The chairman of the House subcommittee investigating the Gauley Bridge project; "Dunn" and "Marcantonio" in the lines following were also members of the committee.

56.6   Third . . . Form]   "The references in the third elegy are to the war in Spain; I went into Catalonia on a quite different errand on the first day, when none of us in England knew there would be war." (Rukeyser's note in *Waterlily Fire*.)

58.12–13   Comtesse de Noailles]   French author (1876–1933) whose fashionable literary salon was frequented by writers such as Proust, Colette, and Cocteau.

59.12   sphere . . . joint]   "The 'sphere at the joint' was a recommendation made by the artist Charles Biederman, when he saw the first cyclotron at Chicago. The recommendation worked." (Rukeyser's note in *Waterlily Fire*.)

60.13   midway to]   When the poem was published in *A Turning Wind* (and reprinted in *Elegies* and *Waterlily Fire*), this passage read "midway travels of."

73.1   Judith]   "The news, as it has progressed this year, has given a wry twist to some of these poems, notably to. . . . . .'Judith,' which was originally suggested by a play by Bertolt Brecht." (Rukeyser's note, dated September 1, 1939, in *A Turning Wind*.)

74.3   Kishinev]   Site of a 1903 anti-Jewish pogrom in Moldavia.

74.3   York]   In 1190, in response to widespread massacres of English Jews, 150 Jews committed suicide in York, England.

75.8   GIBBS]   Josiah Willard Gibbs (1839–1903), American scientist and mathematician who did pioneering work in thermodynamics, vector analysis, and physical chemistry. Son of a Yale Divinity School professor, he spent virtually his entire life (except for three years studying in Europe) in New Haven, Connecticut, first as a student and later as Professor of Mathematical Physics at Yale. Rukeyser's prose biography, *Willard Gibbs*, was published in 1942.

79.11   ANN BURLAK]   Anne Burlak Timpson (1911–2002), American communist activist, labor organizer, and founding member of the National Textile Workers Union. Born the oldest child of Ukrainian immigrants in Bethlehem, Pennsylvania, she lived most of her life in Massachusetts and Rhode Island. She traveled to the South in 1930 to organize textile workers in North Carolina, South Carolina, and Georgia, and was arrested with five others (the "Atlanta Six") for sedition, in a case that was later dropped.

85.3   Ajanta]   Caves discovered in 1819 in the Indian state of Maharashtra, containing Buddhist chapels, monasteries, frescoes, and sculptures dating from c. 200 B.C.E. to C.E. 65. "The frescoes painted on the walls of the Ajanta caves in India, by generations of painter-monks, were made according to a religious principle. This principle is an analogy between space and the space of the body. It involves an acceptance of reality which defines art as other than the changing of reality, the *looking-through* the wall of Western painting. The wall is accepted; the air, the space between the walls and the observer, is filled with creation." (Rukeyser's note in *Selected Poems*.)

87.11   *Les Tendresses Bestiales*]   Bestial endearments.

92.18   Darkness Music]   When first published in book form in *Beast in View*, this poem read:

> The days grow and the stars cross over
> Drawing you nightly
> Along my human love.
> Alone at the vertical wall and wild with tears
> I watch your line of windows.
> Dance of eyes,
> Their constellation steers me from my death,
> Away, persuading me of
> Wavering dawn.
> Breeze of lilac in the sleepless night;
> Here overflown by bells
> Black altitudes,
> And my wild bed turns slowly among the stars.

93.12   The Minotaur]   "The Minotaur is dedicated to Charles Naginski, who shortly before his death wrote the music for a ballet of the same name." (Rukeyser's note in *Beast in View*.)

112.4   *Matthiessen*]   Francis Otto Matthiessen (1902–1950), American literary critic and author of *The Achievement of T. S. Eliot* (1935), *American Renaissance* (1941), and *The James Family* (1947). He committed suicide by jumping from the twelfth-floor window of a Boston hotel. In a suicide note, he described himself as "a Christian and a socialist." His companion of many years, the painter Russell Cheney, had died shortly before.

115.3   Waterlily Fire]   "The time of this poem is the period in New York City from April, 1958, when I witnessed the destruction of Monet's *Waterlilies* by fire at the Museum of Modern Art, to the present moment.
    "The two spans of time assumed are the history of Manhattan Island

and my lifetime on the island. I was born in an apartment house that had as another of its tenants the notorious gangster Gyp the Blood. Nearby was Grant's Tomb and the grave of the Amiable Child. This child died very young when this part of New York was open country. The place with its memory of amiability has been protected among all the rest. My father, in the building business, made us part of the building, tearing down, and rebuilding of the city, with all that implies. Part II is based on that time, when building still meant the throwing of red-hot rivets, and only partly the pouring of concrete of the later episodes.

"Part IV deals with an actual television interview with Suzuki, the Zen teacher, in which he answered a question about a most important moment in the teachings of Buddha.

"The long body of Part V is an idea from India of one's lifetime body as a ribbon of images, all our changes seen in process.

"The 'island of people' was the group who stayed out in the open in City Hall Park in April of 1961, while the rest of the country took shelter at the warning sound of the sirens. The protest against this nuclear-war practice drill was, in essence, a protest against war itself and an attempt to ask for some other way to deal with the emotions that make people make war.

"Before the Museum of Modern Art was built, I worked for a while in the house that then occupied that place. On the day of the fire, I arrived to see it as a place in the air. I was coming to keep an appointment with my friend the Curator of the Museum's Film Library, Richard Griffith, to whom the poem is dedicated." (Rukeyser's note in *Waterlily Fire*.)

133.17   the Academy] The Beaux Arts building at West 155th Street and Broadway, home to the American Academy of Arts and Letters.

138.3   Book of Changes] The *I Ching*, one of the Chinese Five Classics, a book used to predict the future.

140.16   *grenzen der seele*] Limits of the soul.

143.21   Käthe Kollwitz] German artist (1867–1945) who worked in various media, including painting, lithography, and sculpture. Her politically engaged works often depict proletarian life or the horrors of war.

149.13   *Nie Wieder Krieg*] Never Again War, German pacifist group to which Kollwitz belonged and the title of a print she made in 1924.

149.16   "Seedcorn . . . ground"] The antiwar lithograph *Saatfrüchte sollen nicht vermahlen werden* (1942), Kollwitz's final graphic work; its title is taken from Goethe, *Wilhelm Meisters Lehrjahr*, Book VII, Chapter IX.

INDEX OF TITLES
AND FIRST LINES

AMERICAN POETS PROJECT

EDNA ST. VINCENT MILLAY: SELECTED POEMS
J. D. McClatchy, editor
ISBN 1-931082-35-9

POETS OF WORLD WAR II
Harvey Shapiro, editor
ISBN 1-931082-33-2

KARL SHAPIRO: SELECTED POEMS
John Updike, editor
ISBN 1-931082-34-0

WALT WHITMAN: SELECTED POEMS
Harold Bloom, editor
ISBN 1-931082-32-4

EDGAR ALLAN POE: POEMS AND POETICS
Richard Wilbur, editor
ISBN 1-931082-51-0

YVOR WINTERS: SELECTED POEMS
Thom Gunn, editor
ISBN 1-931082-50-2

AMERICAN WITS: AN ANTHOLOGY OF LIGHT VERSE
John Hollander, editor
ISBN 1-931082-49-9

KENNETH FEARING: SELECTED POEMS
Robert Polito, editor
ISBN 1-931082-57-x

MURIEL RUKEYSER: SELECTED POEMS
Adrienne Rich, editor
ISBN 1-931082-58-8

JOHN GREENLEAF WHITTIER
Brenda Wineapple, editor
ISBN 1-931082-59-6